CHRISTIAN FAITH SERIES
Reinhold Niebuhr, CONSULTING EDITOR

DOING THE TRUTH

Doing the Truth

A SUMMARY OF CHRISTIAN ETHICS

by James A. Pike

VICTOR GOLLANCZ LIMITED · LONDON · 1956

PRINTED IN GREAT BRITAIN BY
LOWE AND BRYDONE (PRINTERS) LTD., LONDON, N.W.10

To HORACE W. B. DONEGAN

FATHER IN GOD • COLLEAGUE • FRIEND

with respect and affection

Foreword

This is a book on the relationship of believing and doing, hence the title, suggested by Professor Paul Tillich's sermon of the same name (in *The Shaking of the Foundations*) and for which we are both indebted to the author of the Fourth Gospel. It is written in the conviction that Christian ethics is not simply a lofty set of principles as to what we ought to do but is a way of deciding things based on the unique premises of the Christian faith and a way of doing things because of the unique sources of motivation for the Christian life. The book is an extended footnote on the "therefore" which is St. Paul's transition between the recital of the mighty acts of God and the charge to live as becomes them.

Thus here the classical Christian theology is not argued for, it is presupposed. But the work is not entirely without apologetic intent. To many, in all times, the Gospel has been commended by explication of the ethical implications of it.

And though it is not an exhortation to goodness, nor an "inspirational" book, it is not without pastoral intent. Much of the preparation for the task has been the decade of pastoral counseling in which I have been privileged to engage as a priest, and hence the reflections herein may perhaps be useful to others in their own ethical decisions.

As to the intellectual preparation for the task, I am indebted especially to two whom I am blessed to count as friends and the influence of whose teaching and writing will be evident to many who read these pages: the Reverend Professors Reinhold Niebuhr and Albert T. Mollegen—though neither is to be blamed for any defects herein. The latter reservation also applies to the Reverend Canon Howard A. Johnson, who read the manuscript critically. I also profited much from the stimulus of the students to whom I have taught Christian ethics and Church-State relations at Columbia. I am grateful to my wife, who encouraged me in the work and assisted in the revision of the manuscript. Mrs. Cecilia Irvine, my assistant, also made a number of helpful suggestions.

The author must confess there is nothing unique in the ideas in *Doing the Truth*. It is frankly an exercise in communication.

JAMES A. PIKE

The Deanery
New York City
St. Andrew's Day, 1954

*The Collect for the Day, Book of Common Prayer: "Almighty God, who didst give such grace unto thy holy Apostle Saint Andrew, that he readily obeyed the calling of thy Son Jesus Christ, and followed him without delay; Grant unto us all, that we, being called by thy Word, may forthwith give up ourselves obediently to fulfil thy holy commandments; through the same Jesus Christ our Lord. Amen."

Contents

A*

DOING THE TRUTH

CHAPTER I

Freedom and Responsibility

Ethics presupposes responsibility and responsibility presupposes freedom. There is no point in analyzing what men ought to do if they are powerless to choose what they will do. If our actions are determined, there is still room for law, for sociology, and for psychology, but there is no room for ethics.

There is room for law, because it is possible under some theories of jurisprudence to view law as the systematic statement of what conduct will result in what consequences. If a man takes the life of another he will under certain circumstances lose his own. And, still assuming determinism, it can be said that the public fact of the law against murder and the reality of the gallows serve among the determinants which press men in the direction of conformity.

There is room for sociology, because we can count men's actions and tabulate them; we can show trends and patterns, entirely apart from whether any of the actions observed were free. Indeed, to be thoroughly consistent, we would have to say

that the sociologist could do no less than engage
putations.

. There is room for psychology, because we ca
cause-and-effect relationships between various det
results without reference to the matter of responsib
man loses his mother, to whom he had been over
marries a widow twenty years older than himself.
much less obtuse provide fruitful areas of analysis
from whether the parties could have behaved othe

To the degree that ethics is anything more than l
and psychology—and if it is nothing else, then there is no such
thing as ethics—its distinctiveness lies in its necessary recognition of, and concern for, the responsible formation of intentions
and the free perseverance in the same as they are translated
into action.

Hence the question of freedom is at the threshold as we enter
upon a consideration of Christian ethics. Upon a positive answer
to the question depends the validity of the whole enterprise. But
more than that: upon the nature and extent of human freedom
depends the very shape of the ethical system, especially at such
vital points as the way in which the actor should inwardly view
his own acts, and the resources for a change of direction.

Are we free? Those who answer no can readily produce
illustrations showing we are determined. If the question is posed,
"Are we determined?" the answer has to be yes, but this does
not mean that the answer to "Are we free?" is no. Conditioned
as we may be by factors beyond our control, if there is any freedom at all, then there is responsibility—and hence ethics. So
we should first turn our attention to the limits on freedom upon
which both the determinist and the voluntarist can agree; thus
the ultimate question can be put in proper focus.

Some of the limitations on freedom are obvious, some not
entirely so. Most apparent are physical limitations and limitations of mental capacity. A man can think about going to Mars,

indeed may very much want to go. But—in this generation at least—he can't go there; hence to this extent he is not free. A cripple may not become a football star, a moron a nuclear physicist. Obvious as this is, it is sometimes forgotten by libertarians in the political and economic field as they recite the opportunities untrammeled freedom affords. Equally unrealistic are certain forms of American idealism, especially the "every-boy-can-become-President" type.

Then there are limitations imposed by the actions of others (leaving open the question as to whether they in turn are free or determined). A man's name is willfully blackened by another. If we assume that his traducer is widely believed, certain doors will be closed to him—regardless of his desires, his efforts, his merits. The same is true of the blameless acts of others. Five minutes before X applies at the ticket office for a lower berth, Y reserves the last lower on the train. X is not free to travel to the given destination by lower berth on that train, whatever freedom may be left to him.

Too, similar limitations may be imposed by one's own past actions (again whether free or determined). A criminal record, whatever one's degree of repentance and reform, may well close out a man from certain positions of trust. And, especially during the present tension over the communist threat, a past sympathy for left-wing causes or companions may narrow one's possibilities of present service, in government, education, or industry. Obvious, but contradictory to the common American assumption that one can always make a new start.

And sheer accident or poor timing of human plan and natural event may bar certain fulfillments. A New Yorker may not be free to speak in Chicago a given evening because the plane on which he intended to travel is grounded by below-minimum ceilings. Obvious, but contradictory to the common folk aphorism, "When there's a will there's a way."

So much for outer factors. More subtle, but no less inescapable, are inner factors which bear on behavior. The force of these factors has been more evident since depth psychology has come to the fore. In addition to consciously recognizable factors such as habit and ideological bias, there are the unconscious forces at work—some destructive, some integrative in effect. The sources of these inner urges are partially traceable to one's past and the impact of others upon one; partially they are untraceable. But to the extent that they operate a man is not free, at least in terms of rational choice.

If we tally up all of these ways in which behavior is affected, especially in application to a particular decision, it would seem that there is no room left for freedom. As a man looks back on anything he has done and seeks to answer the question, "Why did I do it?" he can usually answer it in terms of cause and effect. This is so even if he leaves the unconscious factors out of account. In cases where through psychoanalysis or otherwise he does understand something of the forces operating in the depths he is even more likely to believe that what he did was necessitated by one or more factors.

Looking backward, we may feel bound, yet looking forward, we always feel free. How often we weigh issues back and forth, sometimes even making lists of factors pro and con, taking for granted our power of choice. Even when we say, "There's nothing else I can do," or "I just have to do it," we are conscious that *the "I" is deciding* that there is only one possible course of action. And one reason we so often wrestle with decisions is that we feel instinctively that we are responsible for what we decide and fear we will feel either remorse or guilt or both if we decide wrongly.

Analysis of these two responses—remorse and guilt—provides clues to the mystery of freedom.

Remorse is more complicated than chagrin or regret. We can feel the latter of the two emotions even when we obviously had no part in the causation of the unwanted result. But remorse involves a sense that the result was not necessary and could have been different had we decided differently. Though the two states of mind may concur in regard to a given situation, yet they are distinguishable: We can feel remorseful as to decisions about which we do not feel guilty. We can even feel remorseful that we did not "take the easy way out"—the taking of which would have made us feel guilty. And we can feel guilty about decisions as to which we feel no remorse, unable to regret that we did what we did, yet feeling guilty about it.

Now of course *feelings* of guilt or remorse are not infallible clues to reality. There are times we think that things might have been different, when they could not in fact have been so. There are times that we feel guilty, when by any objective standards we were in fact not. In other words, there is such a thing as a "guilt complex." But the universality of feelings of remorse and guilt certainly makes it at least plausible to assume that in general they correspond to a reality. And that reality is freedom and consequent responsibility.

To sum up this point: Looking forward toward anticipated conduct, we do in fact feel free to decide yea or nay, and we fear that we will feel remorseful or guilty if we decide wrongly. Looking back on our conduct, we can often explain it by factors which would seem to indicate that we are determined; yet, frequently enough, we do feel remorse or guilt, indicating that even in the backward look we are conscious of a sense of responsibility—a sense that is grounded in freedom. The resulting paradox is this: starting from an analysis of factors which have borne upon decision, we end up with the conclusion of *determinism;* starting with the consciousness, that is, the inner experience of freedom, we are left with the conclusion of *voluntarism.*

How can we resolve the paradox? One way would be simply to say that we are not as free as we think, but we are somewhat free. Yet this is rather imprecise and incapable of verification. It does not leave us a definition of the area in which we are free, i.e., the area in which ethics can in fact operate. Perhaps there is another way to preserve the truth in both sides of the paradox.

Every man values some things and fails to value others. And the things which he values line up in a priority scale. A man may value both money and his wife, but he may value the first more than the second. When there is a conflict between an opportunity to acquire the first and to nurture love for the second this man will choose in only one way. So, too, a man may be loyal to his church and loyal to his club, but when his club holds an outing on Sunday morning he may place the latter above the former as a claim upon him. Of course, we can not always know of a given person just what his priority scale is; indeed, he may not know just what it is himself. He may think he is operating by one scale and actually be operating by another. The man who says, "I always live by the Golden Rule," may in fact operate by a rule whose metallic metaphor may be more aptly "brass" than "gold." But if we did know all about the behavior pattern of a man we could pretty readily set down in order his scale of priorities.

The values which hold a priority of considerable eminence in a man's life can quite properly be called his "gods." It is interesting that the Old Testament never concerned itself with atheism. Rather it was concerned with *idolatry,* that is, the worship of false gods. We think of an idol, or false god, as the worship of something conceived as a personality, perhaps resident in a statue or stone. But actually in primitive religions idols represent more than this. The figure or image represents an aspiration of man. An obvious example is afforded by the Baalim, or fertility gods, of the Canaanites. That they were the highest gods meant that fertility (of animals and crops—and of human beings to tend the same) was the highest value in that culture.

Now, as well as then, sometimes the idolatry is *monolatrous,* that is, there is definitely one value which is the top god. Often it is *polytheistic* to all appearances; yet at a time of testing (a flat conflict between two values which heretofore had both seemed to be at the top) which is really the top god usually becomes evident. If it does not, the man cannot decide and he is torn.

But to the extent that the man is able to decide he will inevitably decide in the way his priority scale of values requires.

We are here talking about what a man's priority scale really is, not what he thinks it is or what he professes it to be. There is an important difference here, as we have seen. That is why a biographer can better estimate what his subject is really like from his behavior in crisis than from his press releases or memoirs. Looking closely at the will of a man, we will see that he decided in a given instance because there was a preponderance of factors on one side as against the factors on the other side. The valuation given to each factor depends upon his *a priori* commitments to values. As to the given decision he could do no else.

Thus it would appear that there is no freedom as to individual decisions about the conduct of our lives. We will inevitably *do* what we *are*. But, while there is no freedom as to particular decisions, history is replete with instances of men who have been changed from what they were, whose aims and ambitions are altered. This is called *conversion*. Sometimes it has been dramatic; sometimes it has been a gradual process; but we would rule out much that is significant in human history if we did not recognize the reality of such change. The make-up of the converted man does not necessarily change. Indeed, his skills, his methods, his manner, and his basic drives may remain much the same, but the objectives which he seeks to serve—through his abilities and limitations—may be radically altered. St. Augustine is an obvious example. The same brilliance is there, the same "all-outness" for the objective is there, and many of the same faults are there; but what he was living for changed; the meaning of his life changed, and thus his conduct changed. We will consider the nature of conversion more fully in Chapter VII. It suffices to say now that such experiences have been common enough among the great and small of mankind to provide a real pointer to what is the true realm of man's freedom. Of course even here a man is not completely "on his own." Factors from outside of him—the collapse of the old gods, the example and influence of others, and the grace of God—all play their part, but ultimately a man decides what he will be *for*. That this is the real area of freedom is suggested by the fact that it is as to this very matter that a sense of guilt is most intense. If a man has done a shabby thing he is not so much ashamed of the particular act as he is ashamed of the fact that he is the kind of person who could do such an act. He is mortified at the recognition which a particularly conspicuous malfeasance suggests: that he is the sort he is, that he wanted lower things more than higher ones.

In other words, within limits, we are free to choose our gods. Apparently we are free as to nothing else. Thus ultimately the *only true freedom is religious freedom*. This leads quite naturally to a broader consideration of the relationship between religion and ethics.

CHAPTER II

Religion and Ethics

If a man's value pattern represents the hierarchy of his gods, it is obvious that every man has a religion. There are no atheists—in fox holes or otherwise. Men are customarily divided as to whether they think religion is a good thing or a bad thing. Actually both groups are right. A religion can be good or bad—or less good or less bad. When a lady says, "My husband is very religious, though he never goes to church," she probably means that he displays in his life certain aspects of the Judaeo-Christian religio-ethical code. But whether he does or not, her statement is right. He has some religion—whether or not it is the one that he thinks he has or not. For he has a scale of values.

Hence the relation between religion and ethics is inevitable. The moment we move beyond the realm of what a man *does* to what he does it *for* we are forced to a consideration of what a man's true destiny is, and this in turn rests on premises about what the meaning of the whole of reality is. From time to time it has been asserted that all such ultimate questions can be dispensed with by a "scientific" ethics. But in this realm, no more than in physics, can science set what its own goals are.

In the realm of physics this is fairly obvious. Pure scientists can tell us what the results will be from splitting the atom. Applied scientists can make a bomb that actuates these results. But neither type of scientist can tell us—from the resources of science—under what circumstances we ought to drop such a bomb. A scientist may have a very sound opinion on this, but when he offers it he doesn't offer it as a scientist. Science deals with the "is's," not with the "oughts" or the ultimate meaning of things which lies behind the "oughts."

It will be countered that careful observation can tell us the results of certain types of conduct and show that certain types are desirable, other types undesirable. But sometimes "one man's meat is another man's poison." It may be desirable for me to steal another man's $2500 in order that I may have a new car, but it is obviously undesirable from his point of view. But, it will be argued, what is meant is the greatest good of the greatest number. The moment that such a principle as this is introduced we have gone beyond the realm of science and chosen a norm to be received by faith, if at all. And many intelligent people have not in fact received it. Some prefer the greatest good of their own class (meaning perhaps the thrifty and provident), or of the proletariat, or of those of their own race or blood (e.g., a generation ago, the German *Volk,* or, today, the Afrikaans). Some simply prefer their own advantage or that of their family (sometimes explicitly, sometimes implicitly and contrary to expressed aims). *One can be "scientific" about assessing what actions lead to fulfillment of given objectives, but the choice of those objectives is beyond the realm of science.*

There are those who assume that if something is beyond the realm of scientific inquiry it is nonexistent, unknowable, or unimportant. This conclusion, too, is a conclusion of faith: no one can prove that something is nonexistent, no one can prove that something is unknowable, and to assert that something is unimportant is to make a value judgment that science as such is incompetent to make.

As a matter of fact, such a judgment is belied by the very conduct of the person who makes it. Let us take the case of a secularist scientist, described by himself as "unreligious," who claims to take nothing on faith. First of all, he gets up every morning and goes to his laboratory. This is on the assumption that the search for truth is important (he cannot wipe this out by simply saying he does it to earn a living: many a "pure" scientist would prefer to do this very thing at a lesser income than to go into industry at a bigger income to engage in more "practical" feats). Second, he deals with phenomena on the assumption that the phenomena exist. We all operate on the basis that there is reality outside of our own minds (however colored it may be in the process of reaching the mind through the senses), yet this is an assumption which science cannot prove. As far as *proof* goes, all with which we think we are dealing externally may be pictures within our own heads. And, third, the same scientist will be as cross as the next fellow at the man who, in an attempt to speed around him, rips his fender or tries to get ahead of him in a queue. Thus we see that the man who claims to operate on no premises and to limit himself to what can be proven by scientific observation is in fact operating on at least three unproven assumptions (plausible as they may be), namely, that truth is worth-while in the world, that there is external reality outside our minds, and that people ought to behave in certain ways in relation to their fellows.

We cannot criticize this secularist scientist for making these assumptions: so do the rest of us. But we can fault him for claiming that he makes no assumptions. And it is with assumptions of this sort that religion is primarily concerned: the nature and meaning of the universe and the meaning and purpose of man's life. The judging of such assumptions as to their mutual coherence, and the explication of them as to their applicability, ultimately forces us back to questions as to the source and destiny of reality—spiritual and physical. And the answers that we give as to values here and now depend finally upon the long-range view we take—backward and forward—of the meaning of the whole show. And this involves us in religion—or more specifically, as thought about the matter is systematized, in theology. It is theology, regardless of the answers that we give to these questions. It is still theology even if it is believed that *matter* is the ultimate reality: because then matter is God. Or, if our religion is a humanistic one and we believe that *man* is the most important thing, then we have thereby deified man, and the system of thought by which we reach this result and explicate it is a theology.

But whatever our theology and the ethical applications which flow from it, the matter does not end there. No matter how strict or loose a man's ethics, there are times when he does not keep to the standards he purportedly has accepted. The gap between the ought and the is, wherever the line of the ought is drawn, is *sin,* and the resulting condition is usually a sense of guilt. True, those with less orthodox theologies generally do not like the word "sin." They do not like it because they reject certain implications which have been attached to the word in traditional Christian theology; they may reject, for example, the idea of eternal punishment by an offended God. But, regardless of the validity of these cognate doctrines which many Christians hold, some word is needed to stand for noncompliance with one's ethical standards. And "sin" is just as convenient as any other. But, no matter what we call this measure of nonconformity with one's own ethics, a sense of guilt almost inevitably accompanies it. There are a number of ways of relieving the anxiety thus caused. These means will be considered in more detail later. For the religious Jew or Christian the means will be the grace of the forgiveness of sins. Those who recognize no authority higher than man deny responsibility or feel that they can relieve the sense of guilt by greater moral endeavor. Whatever the system of thought that operates at this point, it is trans-ethical. Again there are involved certain assumptions about the nature of man's relationship to his world and to his fellow men. However large mere ethics may loom in the norms of what we ought to do, we have definitely left ethics and entered the realm of religion when we consider how we can accept ourselves when we haven't kept the ethics. If, as part of a system of self-acceptance (whatever scheme it may be), we resolve to do better in the future, we are brought right to the question of motivation. What the resource is for changing our patterns of behavior, what is (to use Professor Spurrier's phrase) the "power for action" is again a trans-ethical question. The norms of human life are one thing; the dynamic for human life is another. The latter is ultimately religious in its context.

The reason why it is necessary to labor these points is that many people live along with ethical norms, with some resources for keeping them, and with a rough-and-ready mode of self-acceptance, but give very little conscious thought to religious questions and are in very little touch with religion as ordinarily conceived. It is part of the folklore of our land that "a man who does not go to church can be just as good as one who does." It would be foolhardy to enter any general denial of this proposition. First of all, as it applies to individual cases, it is obviously something impossible to prove one way or the other. We cannot measure a man's conduct very successfully, especially since an important part of any serious system of ethics, as we shall see later, has to do with inward disposition and intention. Then there is another reason: Observance as to external conduct does not take into account the natural proclivities or weaknesses (with or without espoused religion) in those being observed. A passage from C. S. Lewis is relevant here:

Christian Miss Bates may have an unkinder tongue than unbelieving Dick Firkin. That, by itself, does not tell us whether Christianity works. The question is what Miss Bates's tongue would be like if she were not a Christian and what Dick's would be like if he became one. Miss Bates and Dick, as a result of natural causes and early upbringing, have certain temperaments: Christianity professes to put both temperaments under new management if they will allow it to do so. What you have a right to ask is whether that management, if allowed to take over, improves the concern. Everyone knows that what is being managed in Dick Firkin's case is much "nicer" than what is being managed in Miss Bates's. That is not the point. To judge the management of a factory, you must consider not only the output but the plant. Considering the plant at Factory A, it may be a wonder that it turns out anything at all; considering the first-class outfit at Factory B, its output, though high, may be a great deal lower than it ought to be. No doubt the good manager at Factory A is going to put in new machinery as soon as he can, but that takes time. In the meantime low output does not prove that he is a failure.*

Thus it is impossible to compile general statistics which will be meaningful in a conclusive sense as to the relation of religion and behavior.

But we are generally found using some standard of goodness in the judgments we make along this line. The judgment which the folklore quoted above makes usually means that the Judaeo-Christian ethics are as well observed by those who do not espouse the Judaeo-Christian faith as by those who do. So spelled out, the conclusion becomes somewhat less plausible. The suppositions underlying pedagogy fall to the ground if we say that people are affected in no way whatsoever by the principles upon which they concentrate. To be consistent we would have to conclude that a study of civics is useless in making better citizens and that the study of art appreciation has no bearing upon people's actual appreciation of art. If these inferences are to be rejected, then it is reasonable to suppose that concentration on the world view from which the generally accepted Western ethics arose might have some bearing upon the keeping of such ethics. To turn more specifically to the matter of going to church, it is reason-

Mere Christianity (Macmillan, 1952), pp. 163–64. Reprinted with the permission of the publisher.

able to suppose that keeping in active touch with a group which continually reiterates these principles might help encourage the fulfillment of them in personal lives. If this is not true then the whole theory of social conditioning falls to the ground.

Further, no individual stands apart from his general inheritance. There are those who are good because their grandfathers feared God. There are those who are living by an ethic which is what Dr. Trueblood has called "cut-flower religion." Whether they think much about the religion or not, it has been part of the womb in which their moral life was formed. Such people may even be in conscious rebellion against their religious heritage. Still, in their own behavior and the behavior they expect of other people they are more Christian than they are anything else. They generally respect the minimum negative proprieties, the supports for which in our society can be traced to Christianity. And actually they are usually informed by more than these minima. They exert kindness above the call of duty—and expect it from others. They exercise themselves in a "calling," though they may not recognize the One who has called them; nevertheless they go about their daily work as though it has some long-range significance and they feel "judged" in their failures. Some colorful preachers call those who have lapsed from allegiance to the Christian Church "pagans." But whatever they are, they are not this. Even people who want to be cannot be pagans in our culture. They can behave much worse than pagans, but whether their behavior is good or bad it is always, in whole or in part, in response to or in rebellion against the deep-rooted Christian ethical patterns. There is no denying that as a result of generations of family neglect or due to special environmental "islands" (as we are seeing develop increasingly, for example, in the slums of our large cities) the residual Christian influence may be so slight that the dominant motifs of the lives lived must be otherwise described. This does not mean that the connection between religion and ethics is cut; it simply means that another religion, of which its devotees may be not the least conscious, has taken over. Sometimes it is a crude form of Epicureanism—without the long-range view of planned pleasure which was characteristic of the refined Epicurean of old. What the dogmas of the particular religion may be need not detain us here. But priority scale there is—a god or gods, a simple or complicated hierarchy of values.

Even those emancipated or isolated from the religious roots of Christian ethics cannot entirely escape its impact by the mere fact that the majority of the people in our society are still operating upon them, consciously or unconsciously; hence the expectancies of this majority are so grounded, and accordingly social approval or disapproval, or even legal relationship, is in good part so grounded. A divorced man may think himself a complete relativist in belief and ethics, but he may have to pay for the support of his children. A "hit-and-run" driver may have little personal grounds for interest in a pedestrian whom he has injured and whom he believes to have been at fault, but he will find that society has an interest in this unfortunate person, and the offender may meditate upon the ethical problem behind bars.

It is important that there be a public recognition of the connection between an ethic and its religious roots, so that people's choices of either ethics or religion are made with both sides of the coin in view. One who can sufficiently detach himself from his set of beliefs or mode of life so that he can look objectively at his own set of allegiances and at principal competitive ones may find that, if a particular system of ethics commends itself to him, the doctrinal base therefor is perhaps more worthy of attention than he had realized; or if a particular system of belief commends itself to him he may be open to the idea of accepting the ethical implications of it, unattractive as these may have seemed heretofore. Or, contrariwise, he may be shocked into re-examining unquestioned beliefs when he realizes what the full ethical implications of those beliefs are, or when he realizes what beliefs he is committing himself to by a particular mode of life.

This brings us to a narrowing of our subject. This is not a text on comparative ethics or comparative religion. In an analysis of Christian ethics we must at each point consider the grounding in *belief* of a given category of morals. It is not primarily an apologetic for either the doctrine or the ethics, though the orderly explication of the ethic and the establishment of connections between the various principles of behavior and between them and the categories of belief may well commend, as has been said, both the faith and the ethics.

Thus we turn from the broad questions of the relation of religion and ethics to considerations of the relationship of the Christian faith and Christian ethics. Between them there are three basic connections:

1. Any analysis of moral duty raises a more fundamental question: What is the purpose of life? To discern what man is here for pushes us back to a fundamental theological question: What has God been about in the whole creative process of which we are a part, both as objects and actors?

2. To state the moral law is only part of the problem. Confronted with any kind of rigorous claim, a normal personality reacts in terms of a sense of guilt. How this is to be handled again points us to theology: What is God's relationship to one who has not kept the moral law and knows it?

3. Finally, there is the basic question of the motivation within personality for keeping the moral law and the degree to which God's action impels or inspires our action—again pointing to a theological matter.

Already those accustomed to thinking in theological terms can discern in these three considerations a rough-and-ready suggestion of the Trinity—God as Creator, Redeemer and Sanctifier. And actually Christian ethics does rest on the nature of God as so perceived. But the degree to which this is so, and how this is so, we shall see as we proceed.

CHAPTER III

The Purpose of Life

"Why are we here?" may seem an abstract question to a married man trying to decide what his behavior will be during his wife's absence from the city, to a young man trying to decide what job to take, or to a southern statesman trying to determine his position on segregation in the public schools. Most persons will decide such questions—rightly or wrongly—with little or no conscious reference to the theological question of the nature and destiny of man. But the fact is that a view on that theological question is implied by the decisions they make. And in the long run the soundness of principles and patterns involved depends upon the soundness of the answer they imply as to what man's purpose is.

"Why are we here?" is not just an academic question. There is no one, learned or simple, who does not ask it at one time or another in his life. We are sometimes forced to the question by a deep disappointment, sometimes by the ennui which so often accompanies success. Neither the man whose life has been filled with sensual pleasure nor the one whose life has been markedly disciplined can avoid the question. The former may well be uneasy about what the preoccupation with sense has denied him, the latter uneasy about what his moral rectitude has denied him. Either may be quite unsure what it is he really wants—beyond sensual gratification on the one hand or beyond ethical perfection on the other. As the decades are reached in man's life when it is increasingly difficult to retrace his steps and capture for his life what he may have missed, his uneasiness increases and more frequently it is consciously recognized. This anxiety that he may have missed all or part of the main reason for his earthly existence confronts him with the question, "What *is* the purpose of life?"

The world view underlying some systems of ethics attempts to answer this question in terms of man alone. Christianity does not. Actually it attaches to man a higher dignity than man-centered -isms do, yet it affirms that he is a *creature;* thus the definition of his purpose is not to be found in him alone but is primarily to be referred to what is in the mind of his Creator. Though the analogy breaks down in part because of man's freedom, yet it is suggestive to remember that a machine has no purpose apart from what is in the mind of the engineer who designed it. (If in fact it can be adapted to another purpose that is because of the purpose in the mind of some other person so adapting it.) A machine has no purpose "on its own." So for a Christian, man's purpose is what God's purpose for man is.

We are not able very well to know what the purpose of the various orders of creation are, especially of particular genera and species, and men may reasonably differ as to their conclusions thereon. The purpose of lambs will be viewed differently by vegetarians than by those of more carnivorous inclinations; the purpose of pigs, by Jews and Gentiles. In the limits as to the success of our speculations in regard to the purposes of various species we are reminded of God's challenge to Job: why a hippopotamus? why an ostrich? Whatever may be the purpose of various other items in creation—indeed, if there be any for some, except the extravagant expressiveness of God conceived of as capable of suprarational imagination as well as of rational principle—man stands on a considerably different footing. *Christians believe that God has taken pains to reveal what man's purpose is*. Another volume in this series considers the nature of Revelation, so no more need be said here than that this revelation is not simply a matter of direct word from on high: it is found in the free and divinely inspired response of man seeking the will of God to divinely guided events in history, and principally it is found in—and through—the lives and insights of those who have sought to do His will in prayer, discipline, and sacrificial action. What some of these men have written down and what the Church—the Old Israel and the New Israel—has selected as canonical Scriptures is secondary in authority to the life and experience of the men themselves and those about whom they wrote, and to the living fellowship which has endorsed certain writings because it has found them to ring true to their genuine experience of living out the will of God. But an especially important thing for us to notice in connection with the revelation of God as to the purpose of man's life is that this revelation is conjoined with the revelation of the nature of God Himself. *What God is* is the primary referent as to the purpose of man's life because, unlike the other genera and species, we are made in "the image of God." It is this word from Scripture which is the crucial link between God's purposes and man's purposes. Thus we get at the latter best through an analysis of the former.

What is God's nature in so far as His relation to the world is concerned?

First of all, He is Creator. He not only created the world, He creates it. God operates in and through the evolving order (assuming here the general premise of the evolutionary hypothesis), expressing Himself in manifold and wondrous ways. Ours is, as William Temple has said, "a sacramental universe": what has been evolved and is being evolved is "an outward and visible sign of inward and spiritual grace." At one point along the line there are evolved creatures which, as Le Compte De Nouy has reminded us, are henceforth in on the evolving. What the world is to be like is determined in part at least by our choices as well as His. He has sought to communicate His meaning to us as fully as we have been able to receive it. He is by nature an articulate God: "In the beginning was the Word." The two words *en arche,* which open the Fourth Gospel, can be rendered "as a matter of fundamental principle": the articulateness of God —the Word—is basic in things: ours is a God who speaks. Hence He is creative in *I-thou* relationships (to use Martin Buber's phrase) as well as in the evolving of things and persons.

Second, God is Redeemer. In His relationship to us He is not only a source of norms; He seeks to save those who have not kept the norms, who have come to moral shipwreck, who have to any degree missed the way. Supremely He reveals this character in Jesus Christ, through whom He has translated Himself into the language of human life. What we see in Jesus Christ of God's redemptive activity is a supreme image of how God always has been and always will be toward the sons of men.

Third, God is Holy Spirit. As holy esprit de corps He manifests himself in the fellowship of men who make up the body of Christ and are seeking to make His Kingdom manifest in the world. In this sense He *builds* community but, paradoxically enough, as the Holy Spirit "who spake by the prophets," He *transcends* community and *judges* it.

Such an analysis by no means exhausts the meaning of God. But it does indicate the meaning of God as related to the world, as He has revealed Himself to us.

Now we are made in the image of God. Hence:

1. *God means us to be creative.* We are given the high privilege of being co-sharers with Him in the task of finishing the universe—according to His plan. Genesis reminds us that God

B

is reducing chaos to order. This too is our task. This gives a high dignity to the work of containing rivers by the building of dams, of the sowing and reaping of wheat, of making fine wine out of grapes, in the design of precision instruments—no less than the task of saying our prayers. We are free to turn what order there is into chaos—and are very clever at doing so; but our intended part in His creation is the reverse.

In this is the real ground of individualism. There is a great variety of tasks to be done. Thus we are all created specialists. Men can never really be grouped, never understood in the mass, as far as their relation to the over-all enterprise is concerned. The meaningful expression of individual capabilities—in art, science, or recreation—is connected with the fulfillment of God's will for us. Any system of ethics or government or ecclesiastical polity which thwarts or frustrates the peculiar fulfillment of each individual hinders one of the main purposes of life under God. As we shall see a little later, when we consider the matter of vocation, this does not have to do merely with work. Of real ethical significance is the adage, "All work and no play makes Jack a dull boy." Our sheer joy and ecstasy, our suprarational expressions are part of what individual fulfillment means, as well as the working of reason and disciplined will upon the hard material facts of our existence or upon an orderly spiritual development.

As we have seen above, part of God's creative expression is His articulateness. Our creativity is not meant merely to be our own reasonable working with things or our own exuberant expression. Our articulation of meaning and of joy to other people, the involvement of our meanings with theirs, the expression of our best in the best way, is also part of what it means to be in the image of God. So whether in order or freedom, in self-development or in communication, we are meant to be creative, because God is Creator.

2. *God means us to be redemptive.* This has to do primarily with our interpersonal relationships, with the way we treat each

other. The great variety of human talent implies also a great variety of human limitations. Human freedom implies, as we have seen, the freedom to err—and to err in ways which make us unacceptable to others and to ourselves. God relates Himself to us in our limitations and in our errors and sins, and we in His image are capable of so relating ourselves to others. Indeed, this particular type of relationship is the most distinctive expression of our Christian vocation. This type of relationship is, as we shall see more fully later, the type of love referred to in the exhortation in the First Epistle of John: "God so loved us; we ought also to love one another." This human activity has scope for expression both in one-to-one relationships and in the arrangements we foster in society.

In Jesus Christ the demonstration of God's way with us and the example of man's vocation are merged. In Luke 4:18 we see Him applying to Himself the words of Isaiah: "He hath sent me to heal the broken-hearted, to preach deliverance to the captives, and the recovering of sight to the blind, to set at liberty them that are bruised." All this God does. And all this God expects us to do. God is redemptive, so we are meant to be redemptive.

3. *God means us to live and work in community.* God as Holy Spirit works through the life of the group, in the esprit de corps of "the blessed company of all faithful people," which is the Church, and beyond this He is the genuine inspiration of all wholesome group life. We too are meant to be carriers of the spark of corporate activity. We are meant to be involved in and build up an increasing web of human interrelationship. In this way the effectiveness of our creativity and of our redemptiveness is magnified. But community is not only means, it is end. To appreciate this we should turn from our creation in the image of God to the Christian understanding of man's eventual fulfill-ment. The Kingdom of God is a community of creative and redemptive persons whose lives have become increasingly interlaced and whose talents have received expression in such purposeful ways that all members of the Kingdom have a maxi-

mum relationship to each other, up to the limit of each one's capacities. However, this heightening of community is not at the expense of leveling off of differences but rather rests upon the maximum of the expression of differing gifts focused on the interest and needs of others. But Heaven is not just something that is waited for; it is the pattern of life now. And it is not merely a pattern: the Kingdom has already come to the extent that creativity has expressed itself redemptively in fellowship. Jesus' word that the Kingdom of Heaven is "in your midst," "amongst you," means that in and through Him in whom man as the image of God is supremely manifest, and in and through those united with Him in the fulfilling of God's will, Heaven is already a reality on earth.

Our individuality and our freedom will mean that creativity, redemptiveness, community building will be expressed quite differently by each of us. But each of us is meant to display all three aspects of the human vocation. And each of us in so doing is meant to act as a whole person throughout. While we have a threefold vocation we are not to be divided in personality. And here again we gain a picture of what our integration is to be by returning to the revelation of God. God has related Himself to us in three ways corresponding to His very nature, yet He is one God. When God creates, the whole of God is acting. In Jesus Christ we are in touch with the whole God. When we are reached with the life of the Christian community we are reached by the whole God. This doctrine of the Trinity, which is really the proclamation of God's unity in the face of our threefold experience of God, is the model for us. The ideal view of personality is that man is to be integrated in all of his activity and that primarily in his creative efforts, in his service to others and in his life in community, he is to be pulling in the same direction, with the whole man totally involved withal.

So in the way that God has created us in the image of His triune personality we see the purpose of life, the meaning of our existence. He is Father, Son, and Holy Spirit. We are meant to be *creative, for others, in fellowship*. And as He is one we are meant to be fully integrated as we fulfill our threefold vocation. This is the purpose of man's life.

All of the particular applications mentioned but briefly here will be discussed more fully in the chapters that follow. But it is important that we not miss the forest in examining the trees. Any norms for a particular aspect of ethics have relevance only in connection with this wide-scale purpose of life. God is not interested in our keeping rules for their own sake, nor should we be. He made us for a purpose. The basis for our dignity is that he cares that we fulfill the purpose for which He made us. This is why the basic law of life in both Old Testament religion and New Testament religion—expressed in the *Shĕma* and the "two great commandments"—is the summation of our vocation, the purpose of our life:

Hear, O Israel, the Lord thy God is one God. And thou shalt love the Lord thy God with all thy heart, and with all thy soul, and with all thy mind, and with all thy strength. This is the first and great commandment. And the second is like unto it, thou shalt love thy neighbor as thyself. On these two commandments hang all the law and the prophets.

Here we are reminded that the particular rules depend upon these two great rules and the second of these great rules depends upon the first. Though the second commandment (love of neighbor) is more appealing to a culture drenched with humanism, it is actually unnecessary, except as a reminder. Love of God with whole heart, mind, soul, and strength means the devotion of all our faculties to the fulfillment of our vocation ordained of God. This means creative, redemptive action in fellowship. Such a response to God is what best serves the neighbor. Particular rules which formalize special applications in particular fields of life have their place, but this place is dependent upon and subordinate to the basic claim. The basic claim and the particular rules can come into conflict, as we shall see; here the most difficult questions of ethics arise. Because all is dependent upon the basic claim Christian ethics is a seamless robe: we cannot talk about a part of it without knowing about or thinking about all of it. This is why discussions of particular problems are often so unfruitful: time and patience do not usually permit an examination of the premises of the discussants or the connection of these premises with the surface issues.

Thus before proceeding to particular problems we turn to a fuller consideration of the first great commandment and the basic claim upon us which lies behind it and which in turn rests upon the high calling of those created in the image of God.

CHAPTER IV

God's Claim on Us: Vocation

The first key word then in Christian ethics is *vocation*. It is this concept which distinguishes Christian ethics from any other ethical system. For vocation is a greater thing than law, no matter how nobly the latter may be conceived. Its applications to certain standard situations—in so far as any situation is really standard—can be formulated in laws; indeed, its over-all application is summed up in "the law of love" by the two great commandments. But behind all the particular laws, even behind the law of love, is our calling, which has its grounding in the highest category of reality, namely, the personal. A popular preacher once said, "We don't break the moral law; we are broken on it." This sounds plausible, but actually the underlying concept is more stoic than Christian. From the Christian understanding of things wrongdoing is not so much a matter of breaking traffic regulations as it is a failure to live up to the expectations of someone we respect: it is like "letting down" someone who has counted on us. Thus the moral law rests on the grand premise already considered, that God has chosen us to be co-creators with Him in finishing His creation, in the continuing work of the redemption of men, and in the task of building all men into community.

Our status is that of junior partners in a firm, not that of employees. The distinction in the analogy is not perfect because, as we shall see, the best employer-employee relationships call for a measure of partnership on the part of the latter. But the fact is that the average employee does not share the responsibility with his employers. He keeps the rules connected with the terms of his employment. If he does, he will not get into trouble. Whatever may be certain incidental personal relationships in his association, the fact is the relationship is in essence impersonal. But should an employee be called into partnership in a firm there is a new level of involvement in concern and a responsibility which transcends punch clocks and manuals of regulations. Obviously the latter relationship is the more satisfying. This is not simply a matter of rewards, because actually some employees are better paid than some partners. The essential difference is that between working *for* and working *with*.

This difference changes the character of laws and rules. The employee obeys the rules of an impersonal code; he follows certain rules and norms regardless of whether or not he sees their purpose or their relationship to the over-all objects of the enterprise. On the other hand, the partner has a share in the making of the rules and is constantly reshaping them and interpreting and applying them with direct reference to the firm's aims and objectives. They are for him pre-eminently means to ends, and the ends are the important considerations at every point.

As partners of the living God and sharers in His great enterprise we are bound together in a personal relationship, with shared concern.

When it comes to the *extent* of this claim laid upon us the analogy we have been using breaks down. Whether a man is an employee or partner, only a part of his life is involved in the enterprise, because no human agency is capable of encompassing interests broad enough so that the whole of a man's fulfillment is thereby embraced. To make a contrary assumption as to any human enterprise is to fall into an idolatry which will result in a distortion of life and a failure of fulfillment. In other words, no matter how enthusiastic or loyal a partner may be, he should have "time off," a realm of life that is "his own." But not so in our involvement in the great enterprise. God's service is all-encompassing in its requirement and is the basis of the intended fulfillment of the whole man. There is no "time off." There is nothing beside the service of God that is "one's own business." Why this is so has to do both with the nature of God and the nature of human decision.

God, as Professor Tillich has reminded us, is not a being beside other beings. He is not simply Lord of a particular aspect of life—the "spiritual" or the "moral." He is the ultimate ground of all being; He is Lord of all. This basic premise is challenged every day by the categories of society and through the attitudes of individuals, even of "religious" people. People distinguish the "sacred" and the "secular," and in our universities we tend to think of religion as, at best, a "department." We make distinctions between "principle" and "practice," and especially do we indulge in misleading distinctions between "soul" and "body" and between "spiritual" and "material." Not only is God in and through all things; He is concerned about all things. To subtract certain aspects of life from His reign, such as politics, economics, or personal leisure, is to attempt partially to dethrone Him. While we do not carry through the logic and define other gods as reigning in these particular realms, we in effect do enthrone other gods and violate the first of the Old Testament commandments: "I am the Lord thy God: Thou shalt have none other gods before me." This does not mean that there is not a place for these aspects of life, nor does it mean that there are not, for example, "principles of economics" or legitimate customs which govern our leisure. But it does mean that God—the same

B*

God who is concerned for personal virtues of piety and chastity and interpersonal norms such as honesty and kindness—also stands in judgment over political systems, over the economic order, over the use of all of our time, whether we regard it as leisure or work, public or private.

Made in His image, we are to have as broad a concern as He has. This leads us to the role of human decision. *Every decision we make is for or against God.* The decision and the action consequent upon it either furthers or delays the fulfillment of his aims in some particular realm of life. The furtherance or the impairment may be slight (or seem to be so: one never knows the consequences of even an "inconsequential" action). Thus every decision we make matters to God.

It is important to note *how* it matters to God. It is not that He is interested in each individual act in terms of a personal judgment of us, a sort of "keeping score" as though this life were a series of tests of our character. Each decision matters because it bears on the final outcome of things. This does not mean that God may not overrule the results of our decisions or inspire other persons so to do. It does not mean that the shape of any aspect of things to come is dependent solely upon us. He has a wide variety of resources for the accomplishment of His purposes and is never dependent upon any one of us in any exclusive sense. But the shape of things to come is nevertheless influenced by every single decision we make. The "timing" of the completion of His creative, redemptive, and community-building work, if not the very nature of its completion, does depend, in part at least, on decisions we make.

In short, then, the claim is a total one. There are no moral neutralities. There are no areas in which we are free from His judgments. We are free to do His will or not, to be sure. But we are never free from the problem of doing the will of God. Our decisions in the secrecy of the ballot box are religious and ethical decisions. Our stewardship of time is a religious and ethical matter. This latter most certainly does not imply that there is to be no leisure, no "fun" in life. Relaxation and rest are a part of God's scheme for us. First, for an obvious "instrumental" reason: it better preserves and prepares us for other aspects of His service. But more than that: He rejoices in our joy. Enjoyment by men of the beautiful and wonderful world that He has made is one of the *ends* of creation; it is not merely a *means*. The warmth of the sun, the tang of sea spray, the excitement of new sights, smells, and tastes, the ecstasy of sensual expression and fulfillment are part of what He has meant for us to have—all within the limits of each particular man's vocation.

In the distribution of our time—as between various activities, causes, and persons, in the decision to back this and not that, to focus on this and not on that—we are always deciding for or against God and His will. This is true whether a man is trying to decide on the ministry or the law as his lifework or whether he is trying to decide between working on a speech or playing Scrabble with his children (and we must not forget that there are situations in which the latter and not the former may be the will of God).

This approach may seem too rigorous, but we must remember that any contrary view means that there are areas of life in which God is not interested or as to which He is not the Lord. Some may cry "perfectionism," but here we must be particularly clear. We can hardly endorse the views of perfectionists who have a naïve optimism about the likelihood of perfect performance of individuals and of group performance in society especially. Also, we should, of course, eschew a perfectionism which does not go beyond ethics and does not take seriously (as does God) the redemption of the imperfect in this world. But when it comes to stating *what the law of God is,* and what the scope of vocation is, we may not be less than perfectionists. The logic is clear that every decision is for or against God. And more than logic, we have our Lord's word for it: "Be ye perfect." He ties it to the fact that we are in the image of God and meant to behave as He behaves, in the brief but conclusive analogy: "Be ye therefore perfect, even as your Father which is in heaven is perfect." (St. Matt. 5:48.)

Some may feel that this will lead to inaction for fear of mistakes. There are two answers to this. *Not to act is to act.* Not to further a particular cause because we are not sure is to lend our weight to the opposite. Perhaps that is what we are vocated to do, and inaction may be the best way to do it; but by inaction we have decided—though we may think we have not decided. A second answer is more kindly. Obviously we are not infallible in our decisions as to what may be the will of God; we are not expected to be. Though we are made in the image of God we are finite, not infinite. In fact, the tendency not to recognize the fact that we are finite and fallible is a good part of what we mean by "original sin." Our finitude is not sinful, but to fail to recognize it is. What is asked of us is not an objective rightness in every decision; a man who could achieve this would not simply be serving God, he would *be* God. What is asked is *purity of heart.* "Purity of heart," Søren Kierkegaard reminds us, "is to will one thing." And this is what Jesus means by a man's eye being "single." This is not a simple thing, considering the complication of man's nature and the variety of his internal motivations and the external pressures upon him. But it is a more achievable thing than objective rectitude. Quite simply, it means that we are to be for God in the decisions we make. It means that we are not to be for (in any final sense) any other god, that is, any other aim or interest. A man may indeed further particular aims and interest but only for God's sake, that He may be Lord over all. He may be wrong as to what is God's will—because he doesn't know enough, or because his reasoning doesn't work well enough, or because of the distortion of the mores around him, or because of unconscious factors created by his own past bad decisions and false allegiances. All of this may affect his judgment. As important as the desire to do the will of God is a recognition of the tentative and contingent character of our judgments as to what is the will of God. But that in all that we do we are bound to *seek* to do the will of God is fundamental in the light of His all-embracing concern and the all-embracing claim made upon us.

It is on these terms that God is judge. In the words of the ancient and familiar prayer, it is He "unto whom all hearts are open, all desires known, and from whom no secrets are hid," Whom we ask to "cleanse the thoughts of our hearts." Thus it is that this prayer is called the "Collect for Purity": purity of heart is to will one thing.

Such an all-searching judgment, such a total demand, is meant by God as the foundation for the dignity and significance of each of us in the eternal scheme of things. But more often than not it is seen by men as a burden. Thus all through the history of the Church, of the Old and the New Israel, men have sought to delimit the scope of such a vocation. The very natural and appropriate effort to develop particular codes of law has usually resulted in the proclamation of a lower law than the 100 per cent claim. This has required two special roles among God's servants. The *priests* codify the applications of the claim according to the best insights they know, and men (including the priests) very readily come to assume that this is all that is expected of them. Then *prophets* are raised up to proclaim that this isn't enough and, in fact, swing over in the other direction and show contempt for the codification. Thus Micah says, ". . . and what doth the Lord require of thee, but to do justly, and to love mercy, and to walk humbly with thy God?" (Micah 6:8.) Actually these ends have been the object of the particular rules governing particular aspects of conduct, in his day or in any other, but the false assumption that such rules cover all is the target of his overarching proclamation. So, too, as to the customs surrounding worship: There is nothing wrong with forms of worship, such as the use of incense, if it is helpful to men's receptivity to the presence of God and the conviction that their prayers truly ascend to Him. ("And in every place incense is offered to my name." [Mal. 1:11.] "Let my prayer be set forth in thy sight as the incense . . ." [Ps. 141:2.]) But the tendency of men to assume that when they have offered incense and the like they have fulfilled the law is rebuked by an extreme statement like, "Bring no more vain oblations; incense is an abomination unto me. . . ." (Isa. 1:13.)

The issue in our Lord's time was centered around Phariseeism. In so far as He can be categorized in terms of positions of His day He was a Pharisee; that is, He was on their side in terms of moral seriousness and the attempts to do the will of God in the manifold activities of life. But they often failed to transcend their rule-making because—though much more morally rigorous than their neighbors—they tended to assume that when they kept the particular rules they were righteous. Jesus' objection to the Pharisee was not that he fasted twice in the week and gave tithes of all that he possessed. (St. Luke 18:12.) These are good things and things which our Lord directed us to do. His objection was that the Pharisee thought that when he had done these particular things (and kept similar rules) he had done all that was required of him, when, as a matter of fact, the whole realm of inter-personal relationships and of vocation in the broader sense of the word was largely untouched by such rules. So with the rich young man who had kept the comandments "from his youth up"; Jesus was all for this, but a great deal more was called for.

This has been the issue over and over again in the history of the Church. Especially was it an issue at the Reformation. By this time the load on the average Christian had been lightened by the distinction between the "precepts" and the "counsels." Something involving an approximation of the 100 per cent claim was involved in the *counsels,* meant for the "religious" (i.e., monks and nuns): the vows of poverty, chastity, and obedience were meant to express an "all-out" acceptance of a total claim upon life. But for others, including the bulk of the clergy—not under such vows—the *precepts* applied. These were the Ten

Commandments and the "precepts of the Church." Not to fulfill them was sin, but the decision as to other matters was in the area "above the law," literally *supererogation*. A man *need* not do more than the precepts to avoid sin. To be sure, the Church was happy to have him do more and indeed encouraged him to do so; but, since he was not required to do them, for these works of supererogation he gained extra merit. To visit the sick, to give to the Church, to make a pilgrimage, to say prescribed prayers gained merit which could be counted against the "demerits" and penalties—in this life and in the life to come—imposed for sins; that is, for the violation of any of the precepts.

This is the deeper issue underlying the surface question of "indulgences" which figured so prominently in the Lutheran Reformation. Since many good people, notably the saints, died with a balance of merit, because of an abundance of works of supererogation, this was not to be lost but saved in a "treasury of merits." Those whose balance was "in the red" could draw on this treasury of merits (which included our Lord's abundant merits as well as those of the saints) through prayers or acts prescribed by the Pope. The spreading around of the results of goodness in the community of the faithful was not the problem (this is always a result of goodness in community) but rather the fact that there were no extra merits to be spread around, at least in so far as works of the saints were concerned (and as far as Christ's merits are concerned, His grace is *free,* the New Testament makes clear). As for "works of supererogation," no man, saint or otherwise, could have done more than God willed for him to do; and to do less than the will of God is sin, whereas to do the will of God is not an extra performance. As the Anglican Articles of Religion state it, "Voluntary Works besides, over and above God's Commandments, which they call Works of Supererogation, cannot be taught without arrogancy and impiety: for by them men do declare, that they do not only render unto God as much as they are bound to do, but that they do more for his sake, than of bounden duty is required: whereas

Christ saith plainly, When ye have done all that are commanded to you, say, We are unprofitable servants" (Article XIV).

Thus the Reformation was, among other things, the reassertion of the absolute claim of God upon the whole of life. While in many quarters of the Reformation the special vocation of the "religious" was unwisely circumscribed, yet the reformers and their successors were wise in their insistence that the "religious life" was not a higher vocation, since all men in their several callings were called to perfection. Hence the implicates: the sanctity of the common life, the priesthood of all believers.

Lest the stand we take on this issue be an occasion for self-congratulation by modern heirs of the Reformation, we must remember that the same tendency to limit the demand to the current codification thereof has been repeated since in Protestant cultures. All too often it has been assumed that the good man is the man who keeps the commandments plus a few precepts (perhaps —but not necessarily—including one of the medieval ones, namely, the requirement of churchgoing, and including a few novel ones such as, "don't drink," "don't smoke," "don't dance"). Meanwhile the great bulk of his life, his business ethics, his labor relations, his political attitudes, his social mores, remains untouched—indeed, often impervious—to the claim of God or the claims of fellow men. After all, the claim that the Church should have nothing to say about public issues is most commonly heard on the lips of *Protestant* laymen. The chief example of religious sanctions for segregation is provided by a Reformed Church (the one in South Africa). The pervasiveness of the tendency to limit God's claim on us is one demonstration of the validity of the concept of original sin.

CHAPTER V

The Ethic and the Ethics

For the Christian more fundamental than law is vocation. Thus it is that the basic law, the two great commandments, is as broad as vocation. This law does not specify what particular acts constitute love of God or of neighbor; it does not specify what is the measure of "whole strength" or "whole mind," nor does it specify who is embraced by the phrase "one's neighbor." The terms of the law of love are such that it leaves no doubt as to the *totality* of the claim: nothing is to be held back from God's service, and, as the parable of the Good Samaritan makes clear, a man's neighbor is anyone in need whom a man is able to help.

Obviously such a broad law does not give us the rules for a given man's life. There are competing claims among the avenues of service. For example, it is a good thing to worship God in church, and a housewife could worship God day in and day out, with her whole strength, leaving her husband and her children to fend for themselves. Yet this well might not be the will of God for her. Or a man could devote his entire capital of five thousand dollars to helping a worthy boy through college (the latter's need would certainly qualify him as a neighbor under the parable) and thus be unable to pay his bills. In our Christian service we cannot, like Sancho Panza, go off in all directions at once. To assume that we can is a failure to recognize our finitude and can lead to frustration and disillusionment. The tendency of generous-hearted persons to let *immediacy* be the norm of decision to help is at variance with the overarching claim of vocation, as is, of course, an overcarefulness which results in rejection of crying needs.

Thus the two great commandments do not tell us precisely what to do. As to the negative aspect of the matter, service of God and of neighbor requires that we *not* do certain things. But on the positive side the law of God gives no *explicit* guidance—either in general or as to particular persons.

We have seen that particular rules of conduct have been developed partly to *mitigate* the total claim. But there is valid reason for fresh development in ethical theory and practice, to give guidance as to *how to apply* the law of love, positively and negatively, in particular areas of experience. Obvious examples are the Ten Commandments and the precepts of particular Church traditions. What is the relationship of these latter to the law of love and the overarching sense of vocation?

Suppose a passenger in a taxicab finds on the back seat an envelope containing five hundred dollars. The name on the envelope indicates that it belongs to a prominent man of considerable means. Now there are sets of circumstances which could be conceived in which it would appear that greater good would be achieved if the finder did not return the money. He could weigh out the relative advantage of the sum to the owner as against the value of certain objects to which the finder could put the money. But, in fact, the average honest person would not go through all this; he would simply take the steps necessary to turn in the money or to return it directly to the owner. The explicit commandment, "Thou shalt not steal," will have served to decide the issue forthwith.

Likewise, though it would be possible to be convinced that there were more advantages in the death of a particular person than in his continuing to live, yet virtually all individuals, regardless of their views or feelings toward another person, have let the simple commandment, "Thou shalt not kill," decide the question, and they do not even enter into a process of evaluation which opens the question of whether or not they should kill another person. While there are circumstances in which to kill would appear to be a right and a duty, normally the question is simply not raised.

To move to the realm of less hallowed regulations, an attentive driver, on seeing a red light, simply pulls to a stop automatically. He does not enter into a colloquy with himself as to the relative merits of proceeding (even cautiously on an empty street) or stopping. He stops. Likewise, as a guest to dinner, he does not, gazing at a bone of a steak left on his plate, compare the advantage of gaining a few additional vitamins by picking up the bone and gnawing on it with the disadvantage of disturbing his hostess. He simply leaves the bone where it is, in spite of the fact that one could conceive of circumstances in which the former suggested course of action might be the right one.

These examples might be explained on the ground that we are so socially and psychologically conditioned that we are in the grip of the customs of our forefathers. Doubtless this is partly the case; but, entirely apart from any absolute quality that one or another of these rules may have, psychologically speaking, we cannot go through life all day long, week in and week out, applying to each decision—major or minor—the broad question of our vocation or the law of love. We need "rules of thumb" which readily decide most matters for us. A complete ethical evaluation of each situation which arises in the course of a day would readily drive a man to distraction and render him impotent for action at all.

In the case of one of the examples used (the red traffic light) the standard decision is an arbitrary one; simply for an easy directness of decision and a reliability about the actions of others this particular device has been settled upon. An independent decision could be allowed in each instance (as in the case of most street corners in the land), or it could have been arranged that cars go on brown and stop on blue. In the case of another example used, the rule of etiquette involved simply reflects what in our time seems the proper delicacy about eating. And at other times (not necessarily less moral) nibbling at a bone has been viewed as a proper—perhaps even a requisite—activity for a guest at the table. Nevertheless, even these two decisions are not divorced from ethics or the total claim on life (since, as we have seen, nothing can be alien to this total claim or removed from its jurisdiction). Supporting the conformity to traffic signals is a more universal norm—respect to law as the basis of solidarity in society; supporting the rules of etiquette is a more basic requirement of sensibility to the feelings of others—though in each case the particular rule involved is obviously a relative one.

Is the same analysis true of the other illustrations—those involving rules against theft and killing? Our first reaction, of course, is that these indeed are absolutes (and we can perhaps be grateful that most people so regard them). Any claim to absoluteness we may have is not rebutted by the numerous violations of each rule. One assumes that a man who steals or kills has a bad conscience about it—or should. Even those who try by statistical analysis to defeat the absoluteness of certain other norms (such as sex mores) do not extend the application to theft and murder; they do not argue that the fact that so many people do these things proves the laws against them are relative.

But serious difficulty is presented by the fact that there are situations (and rather standard ones) in which these apparently universal rules are not applied in society. As far as taking what belongs to another is concerned, seizure of arms in war or post-war "occupation" in the international scene and the exercise of eminent domain in the local scene illustrate more accepted situations in which what belongs to another is taken. The fact that in the latter situation there is compensation and consent of the rest of the community still does not cancel out the fact that what belonged to a man was taken from him. The colloquial phrase, "It was a steal," indicates what is involved. In the case of killing, there comes to mind capital punishment (albeit a debatable tradition), war, and the exercise of the right of self-defense. Are these conditions mentioned *exceptions* to the rule, or is the rule such that it needs to be stated more clearly to exclude these situations? Some translate the commandment, "Thou shall not kill," as "Thou shalt do no murder." This would seem to save this norm from suffering any exceptions to it. But our horror at killing, even in wartime or as punishment for crime, reminds us that we really do not regard killing as a *good* thing under any circumstances. In the situations noted we do not regard the *alternative* as good (not to protect oneself in self-defense, not to defend one's country, etc.). The problem of pacifism will be more thoroughly considered in a later chapter. But, assuming for present purposes the general opinion among Christians that there are "justified" killings, what we have is not an exception to the rules which makes the killing *good* or even neutral in character, but a balance of goods and of evils and a resulting choice of the greater of two goods, the lesser of two evils (though, as we shall see in Chapter VIII, the choice may be, in the situation, *the right thing*).

Let us assume that a man who is beyond draft age is weighing whether or not to volunteer for military service in a war in which his nation is engaged. He dislikes killing as much as the next man and earnestly wishes that the war were not on. But it *is* on and the issues in it are such that he sincerely feels that the victory of his nation (a freer and more peace-loving land) against the enemy (a more authoritarian and imperialistic nation) will be vastly better for mankind. Let us assume further that his responsibilities are such that this particular service to mankind will not involve serious harm to any to whom he may be responsible. Here there is no "rule of thumb" which can settle his decision automatically. Indeed the one "rule of thumb" (the commandment, "Thou shalt not kill"), while representing certainly a factor in the case, is obviously not determinative in a simple sense. What should be determinative is his conviction (which is not an infallible one, as we have seen) that by entering into the fray, or by not doing so, he will be better fulfilling his vocation to God and serving his neighbors (in this case, men of the world as a whole as well as his fellow citizens). There is no explicit law of God or man which tells him whether he should go into service. (Even if there were, and he were embraced within the draft law, that would not be finally determinative, as we shall see in discussing the matter of war and peace.) This basic consideration of vocation transcends all specific laws and, in fact, could result in a decision which violates a specific law (in the case of the draft, obedience to civil authority, should he not go; the commandment against killing, should he go).

Likewise, if a man decides he is *for* capital punishment (whether he should or not—the author is undecided), it is because he believes the benefit to society from so treating proven malefactors outweighs the violence done the individual personalities thereby. Similarly, the justification (where it exists) for self-defense would be that the life of the person attacked is more worthy of saving than the life of the attacker, though few would argue that, apart from this balance, the death of the attacker is a *good* thing. Though people might say, "It served him right," they do not mean that his death is unqualifiedly right, as is indicated by the fact that, were he tried for the attack, he would not receive the death penalty, even if the attack were with the intent to murder.

To turn to another field, "Thou shalt not commit adultery" is one of the commandments and is regarded as a fundamental norm, yet the heroine of the apocryphal book of Judith goes forth from besieged Jerusalem to the camp of the Assyrian commander Holofernes prepared to lie with him that she may have the opportunity of slaying him and thus freeing her nation. (The fact that his intemperance as to the proferred refreshments happily relieved her of the necessity of committing adultery in order to stab him does not change the moral character of her prior decision.) Judith could have relieved herself of the burden of undertaking this hazardous enterprise simply by reciting the commandments. But the tradition of her nobility rests upon the fact that she did not. To her conscience the saving of the people of God from the pagan invader inspired in her a vocation to act in this unconventional manner. Yet the commandment was not thereafter rewritten (to, for example, "Thou shall not commit adultery except to raise the siege of a city"), nor would anyone argue that the adultery or the slaying—as such—would be a good thing. Yet she remains a heroine. Her judgment about her vocation transcended the law—even so hallowed a law as the one against illicit sexual experience, the one against killing. Decisions not unlike hers were made during the last World War by members of the French Underground, whose deeds in service of the hopes of freedom have evoked praise, not condemnation, from quite moral people.

The point is that here we are not dealing with absolute laws: there would be no way adequately to frame series of exceptions to them which would preserve their absoluteness, and in any event, even in the case of the "exception," harm has been done; and thus we are not talking about absolute good *versus* absolute evil, but more good mixed with lesser evil versus less good mixed with greater evil. The point is that the claim of vocation can transcend a given norm, whether it be a biblical commandment, a "rule of the road," or a rule of table manners.

The simplest conclusion to draw is that the particular commandments and rules are not binding but that there is only one rule: the fulfillment of one's vocation under God. And as a matter of principle this conclusion is correct. As a formula, however, it could lead readily to antinomianism and thus to considerable unreliability in the conduct of people. Further, the abolition or disregard of the customary moral injunctions would have a particularly serious effect in the light of the unreliability of human motivations. In our illustrations we have been assuming purity of heart, but the power of rationalization is so subtle that man may desire purity of heart and even think that he has achieved it and still be motivated by factors which have not consciously played a part in his decision. Likewise there must be some meaning to the well-nigh universal acceptance of some of these laws that we have shown nevertheless to be relative. What then is their status in the Christian scheme of ethics?

Here we must review, beginning with the more obvious considerations. First, at the lowest level, whatever may be the fundamental character of the accustomed norms, the violation of them may bring penalties which may inhibit a man in the fulfillment of the highest norm (vocation). A man may sincerely think that he can spend the five hundred dollars referred to better than its owner, but he cannot do so in jail. A man may feel it is better to eat every bit of meat on his plate, including that conjoined to the bone, but such a course of conduct may circumscribe interpersonal relationships which may be more important in the fulfillment of his vocation to God than a slight increase in his protein intake.

Second, as we have indicated, a man cannot afford the time or mental energy to wrestle within his spirit as to every decision that comes along. For his own peace of mind most of his life has to be "standard" in its habit patterns. Third, a great support for the fulfillment of the vocation of other people is reliability in our behavior. That people will behave in certain ways, that they will be both polite and "law-abiding," is depended upon in the decisions people make. Fourth, the commandments protect fundamental values in the personal lives of those constrained by them: their violation damages the actor as well as the other persons affected. Fifth, these laws represent the universal group experience of the race as to what gives an opportunity for the greatest good for the greatest number; i.e., the greatest chance for the most people to be free to fulfill their vocations.

This latter reason represents a weight of judgment which can be rebutted only by the strongest factors in the premises. In other words, to decide to violate the law would call for the most pressing contrary factors and the most objective soul-searching possible in order to bring to the surface all that would argue against purity of heart. This does not mean that the presence of any self-serving factor would throw the decision the other way. Holofernes might have been an attractive man indeed, and Judith might quite naturally have had, consciously or unconsciously, some anticipation of pleasure in the circumstances. Or a conscientious gentleman, weighing whether or not to get into a uniform, may in fact sense both joy and advantage in taking a commission in the armed forces. In neither instance would the factors necessarily throw the decision the other way. But it is rather important that both Judith and the potential soldier have established conscientiously that these were not the reasons for the decision, or at least that the higher reasons were genuine ones sufficient of themselves to contradict the usual norm. In other words, a decision to act contrary to the law need not always be one totally unattractive to us, but the greater the attraction the greater the necessity of the sifting of motives so that we know the decision is on firm ground and that we are freed, as much as may be, from rationalization.

Finally, the ethics of a revealed religion may assume that in those norms which have been consistently proclaimed by the covenanted people of God there is a reflection of what is the general will of God for man. For example, it is safe to say that God generally wills that there be no adultery. What this means, too, is that He wills that there not be situations in which adultery would be an appropriate action. For example, we can assume that He would not will that an alien enemy would besiege a city of another land for imperialistic gains. Judith's necessity of decision presupposes that less than the will of God has already occurred. This is no less so in the case of the potential soldier. In other words, we can assume that commandments against adultery and killing would have an absolute quality in a world in which there were no antecedent evils. In most cases they are decided for even in an evil world (or especially because of the existent evil in the world). But the fact is that in the world in which we live even these most accepted and salutary rules end up being somewhat less than absolute. All that is absolute is the 100 per cent claim of God on each individual life: that we serve Him with full devotion in a sense of vocation; and on this claim (as expressed in the two great commandments) "hang all the law and the prophets": the accepted code of commandments— "the law"; and the norms for the transcendence of these commandments—"the prophets."

This approach does not present an easier ethic, and in most cases it requires us not only to keep the customary rules to the letter but to go beyond them. We are called to perform individual imaginative acts which no ethical "pigeonholes" could successfully encompass (such as saying just the right word to a person who is shy and self-conscious or moving out of the sphere of one's own business or professional life to devote hours to a cause which is unpopular); and we are called to engage in a conscientious weighing of factors which actually contradict what normally are reliable norms, both in the more dramatic situations we have used as illustrations and in the meeting of day-to-day need. (It is this latter which is involved in our Lord's endorsement of the disciples plucking grain on the Sabbath: He would have been against man's organizing his work so that he did his harvesting on a day of worship, but when his followers were in fact hungry on a Sabbath He knew that it would be better for them to have something to eat.) Such an approach to ethics is neither easy nor lax.

In any case it is only this view which maintains the fundamental basis of Christian ethics which we have already analyzed: It is not a set of laws, not even a set of noble and lofty norms. It is obedience to a personal claim and a calling to exercise our share in God's great creative, redemptive, and community-building enterprise. This view of things is the basis for the right kind of individualism, the basis of the dignity of the Christian man. This is the birthright which is the basis of our freedom as the sons of God and as the slaves of no man, of no earthly authority, of no system. To live responsibly within such freedom is our vocation.

CHAPTER VI

The Meaning of Failure: Sin

"Until I knew the law," says St. Paul, "I had not known sin." One reason some people can breezily sum up the whole subject of ethics and religion by saying, "I just live by the Golden Rule," is that they do not grasp what a large demand is involved in the Golden Rule and is implied even more by the full law of love of God and neighbor. The man who can prate about the Golden Rule without any sense of self-criticism has obviously translated it for himself into an easygoing ethic: in short, he doesn't go out of his way to hurt anybody and perhaps does a good deed every day. But once the full scope of Christian vocation is evident to one's mind, a man is myopic indeed if his mind does not turn to the next problem; namely, that of his own failure to keep such a law. Though originally the *Kyrie eleison* was a burst of praise, there is a psychological fitness in the fact that in the Anglican service it is after the reading of the commandments that the people respond, "Lord, have mercy upon us." Knowing the law, we know our sin.

We don't like to think about our sins. But there are only two ways of avoiding the problem of sin: to live up to the 100 per cent claim or to grade down the claim to the measure of our actual behavior. Since we generally don't do the former, we yearn to do the latter. But in sound logic and in Christian teaching we can't really lower the claim. Thus we cannot honestly avoid the problem of sin. Sin is simply the gap between the claim of our vocation (stated as law in the two great commandments) and our actual empirical behavior.

It is not our purpose here to brood over the sins of the world or to beat the reader over the head for his own sins, but rather to see what is really involved in sin. We should consider first the psychology of sin and then what we might call the sociology of sin.

Let us take a real-life situation which should be familiar, with variations, to most pastors. John and Mary had been married for twenty years. During the last fifteen of these John's attentions and display of affection had been rather perfunctory and Mary's responses were likewise. This did not worry either of them very much. They had been preoccupied with the various activities of a middle-class society: John with his business, his club, and his golf; Mary with attending to the home and providing a modicum of entertaining, tending to the children, participating in the activities of the suburban women's club, and carrying responsibilities in a couple of charities. A new employee of John's firm, named Martha, a talented and attractive woman ten years younger than himself, focused her personal charm on John at every opportunity (this was for a variety of motives: she recently had suffered a romantic setback and felt the need of male attentiveness; she was naturally outgoing and friendly, and she was eager to get ahead). John's conferences with Martha from time to time in the office seemed much more exciting to him than times spent with his wife. She drew him out, responded in enthusiasm to everything he said, and he in turn found himself more responsive to her than to his wife and "gave out" more than he had to anyone for a long time.

We need not tarry over the details that led to an affair. John was completely captivated. He made good resolutions from time to time, but they were of little effect since he felt he had more enjoyment in life now than he had had for years or perhaps ever. Mary reactions were hardly counteractive: they consisted of a nagging about the additional time he was spending in the city with his work—a nagging aggravated by a persistent suspicion. Martha's conscience was eased by the fact that it was evident that Mary had become far from an appealing companion to him and because she had been rather shamefully "let down" by a fiancé who had first relieved Martha of her inhibitions about extramarital relations.

Now if we look at the matter in a legalistic way we can simply sum up the whole thing by saying that John and Martha committed the sin of adultery x number of times. But this is to deal with symptoms only. If we turn to the factors obviously underlying the particular acts we can not only see the rationale for the stricture against adultery but can discern also a pattern of omission even more basically sinful and can trace the interaction of sin upon sin. The basic fact is that neither John nor Mary was fulfilling his vocation as a married person. Neither was taking pains to be fully outgoing to the other, spiritually or physically (in fact, it is dangerous to make a distinction here, as we shall see later), not only in the interest of one's best self-fulfillment, but in the interest of the fulfillment of the other. The gods of business success, respectability, standing in the community, hopes for the children, successful competition in both the marts of trade and in the things of suburbia—some of these good things in themselves—had been allowed to suffice for life's meaning.

Assume that we can add to this list the support of—and some attendance at—the local church. But for them this was just one thing among many. There was not an overarching religious allegiance sufficient to challenge the pantheon of gods which were really the final things in their lives. Thus they were not awakened to the fact that part of life was neglected: interpersonal relationships had been perfunctory, and there had been a shriveling up of responsiveness. The lack of responsiveness in each was both cause and effect. This is one reason that one church was wise not long ago to remove from its canon law relating to remarriage after divorce the phrase, "the innocent party in the case of adultery": there rarely is such an innocent party.

Made aware of the vacuum in his life at a time when such an awareness was intensified by the unconscious feeling that the possibilities of such fulfillment had real time limits, John has put himself first in his zeal to "fill out" his life. Again the sin of omission is more basic than the sin of commission. It did not occur to him to think of the fact that Mary's life has been similarly unfulfilled. He did not let his new responsiveness remind him of the possibility that such an ecstatic relationship could, with some initiative on his part, be established with Mary, that he could thus help save her from what was essentially a fairly drab existence, in spite of material plenty and a fair standing in the race for social position and general acceptability.

There is another corollary. Now such understanding and concern as John had for working out the problems of domestic life diminished. Since he could so readily turn to one who received him enthusiastically and "understood" him, his patience or desire to work out the little day-to-day relationships of home life was much impaired. So he simply "closed up," knowing where he could turn for a different kind of atmosphere than that created by the rising tensions. It did not occur to him that the long-standing involvement which marriage represents and which the maintenance of a home implies creates more occasions for adjustments than an affair for which the occasions of meeting had a rather artificially favorable setting, the apparent peace of the latter relationship being due principally to the irresponsibility of the relationship.

Mary's resentments eventually achieved a basis wider than his increasing neglect in terms of time. When he was around, there was no rapport. Home became just a place in which to sleep and, sometimes, to eat. John sought to share in conversation less of his daily life, because there was someone with whom he had already shared it.

To turn back to Martha, a good part of the reason why she was in the situation is found in the previous relationship and the wrong done to her by her former lover. The meaning of this relationship to each could occupy us for some time, but suffice that to say there were complicating factors in which the wrong-doing—particularly in terms of omission—of a number of other people played as causative a part as the make-up of each partner. While both John and Mary were much in need of affection, owing to poor parental influence, neither was very natural about taking the initiative in expressing it and thus was quite ready to respond to someone who had natural gifts for taking such initiative.

Thus we see that we cannot deal with sins in isolation. Sinfulness is a very complicated web in which any given conduct which is less than normative is interlocked with the actor's own past and with the present and past of other people. This is why it is so easy, as we have seen, to make a case for determinism. Every decision that a man reaches can be explained by tracing out all the precedent and cognate factors. While, as we also have seen, this does not in fact rebut the factor of freedom (though it implies limitation on its scope) it does support Kierkegaard's dictum that sin presupposes itself. Every particular sin is due in part at least to previous sins, one's own or those of others (in this case hundreds of little decisions of John and Mary and Martha—and of their parents and companions along the way—decisions made not in a sense of vocation but in the immediate terms of selfish fulfillment, have their part in the present unhappy outcome), and each particular sin is in turn causative of more sin.

This complicated interrelationship is true not only of particular "life stories." Wrongdoing infects the society as a whole. The weakening of the reliability of moral conduct in a culture is not the result of a general decision about general propositions; it is the cumulative effect of particular failures of vocation in particular situations. And in turn these particular failures have been partly the result of previous failures in the life of the actor involved and in the lives of others. Thus it is that John did not come to the particular temptation which Martha presented in a position simply to balance the pros and cons as to the one given choice. He came to a decision as a man with a bad past as far as the fulfillment of vocation is concerned and one much affected by others' bad pasts—and "presents." If we had at hand (and had time to discuss) the history of the wrong decisions of the parents of John, Mary, and Martha and in turn of their parents, etc., all the way back, and of all the persons who affected the lives of any of these people, we could through this psychoanalytic group biography grasp the complication of sin.

This complication is such that we cannot adequately deal with sin simply by focusing attention upon particular sins of particular people in whom we may be interested. This is why, in the personal realm, New Year's resolutions are so impotent. This is why Christian theology makes a distinction between *ad hoc* sin ("actual sin") and the whole complicated structure of evil which historically, sociologically, and psychologically does penetrate the whole human race ("original sin"). The latter is indispensable as a category. But in fact it has been dispensed with in American secular thought and in a good part of American Protestantism for some time, leaving a vacuum in the serious understanding of human behavior.

The reason why "original sin" was discarded in many quarters is that it was widely understood only in its most naïve form, which indeed presents an untenable position. The naïve understanding of original sin is something like this: God gave our first parents an arbitrary commandment not to eat the food of a particular tree. The devil, disguised in the form of a serpent, tempted them so to eat and they yielded to the temptation—first

C

Eve, then Adam. God was angry and punished them, driving them out of the Garden of Eden. But this was not sufficient to satisfy his wrath: he decided to conclude under sin all of their heirs in the human race. Then four or five millennia later He arranged for some individuals to be relieved of the burden of this guilt if they were baptized. It is not surprising that such a tale was rejected out of hand by sensitive people outside and inside the Church. Actually the whole thing was made even less acceptable by the folklore which caused many people to interpret the eating of the apple as the first sexual embrace, a view supposedly buttressed by such texts as, ". . . and in sin did my mother conceive me." (Ps. 51:5.)

But actually original sin is not because of Adam and Eve; rather the narrative of Adam and Eve is because of original sin. The story of the Garden of Eden was developed (perhaps out of previous folk legends) rather late in the history of Jewish literature and is a mythological picture of what was already perceived to be man's central problem. We have already analyzed that problem briefly; let us see how the myth expresses it. First, however, a word about the function of myths in religious thought. People usually think that a myth is something that isn't so. Actually a good myth is the picturing of something that *is* so—generally a complicated and paradoxical truth about a situation which can better be portrayed in a story than in a series of logical propositions. The critical question to ask of such a narrative is not, "Is it historically true?" It may or may not be; such elements of historical truth as it may contain does not destroy its value or pre-eminent function as a myth. The proper question is, "Does it adequately hold together the facets of truth in the situation which it seeks to portray?"

The first thing this myth portrays is what God has wanted man to be: the fact of, and the nature of, man's vocation under God. This myth is set in the context of the creation stories in which God unfolds the various levels of reality and finally man is made in the image of God. The redemptive and community-building functions of our vocation are not yet explicitly indicated, but the creative functions are: man is to name all the animals and is to have dominion over them. The *naming* of things is the charter for the scientific enterprise and leads to *dominion,* which is the charter for technics. What can be named can be controlled and manipulated. In this enterprise man is left free; God could have established the intellectual categories for the understanding of nature and the particular types of controls over it right from the outset. Instead He gives men stewardship over this phase of the completion of the task of making order out of chaos, which task He himself undertook and in which He has made man co-sharer. The true God is the God for Adam and Eve; the divisiveness created by false gods is not yet present in the picture. Thus there is no barrier between God and man. Adam talks with God in the Garden; Adam has no sense of guilt (his nudity is symbolic of this), and the garden setting itself is symbolic of the peace and unity of life.

Now we turn to the other side of the paradox. The serpent tempts Eve. It is important to note the character of the temptation: *Ye shall be as gods.* This is the temptation for autonomy apart from God, the temptation to set up one's self and one's affairs and earthly arrangements as final categories of meaning and devotion. The mysterious figure of the serpent suggests that even from the beginning sin presupposes itself and that already things had gone awry in the universe before man came along. Eve—and, through her influence, Adam—makes a declaration of independence from God, and the problem of good and evil is brought to their consciousness.

The first decision they make is for evil. This is the usual result of self-centeredness. Now Adam's relationships change in three ways. He is separated from God (he hides from God: he doesn't want to "talk about religion," as has been the case of so many since who have not kept God's will). He is also separated by sin from his neighbor: he seeks to place the blame on Eve. ("The woman whom thou gavest to be with me, she gave me fruit of the tree, and I did eat.") And he is separated from his true self as made in the image of God. The guilt feelings are symbolized by the fig leaves: they are telling signs of his spiritual dis-ease.

Now the peaceful garden scene is disrupted: travail has replaced peace. Cain and Abel are born into a disordered world. They reflect the schizophrenic picture. Also made in the image of God, they cultivate the soil and tend flocks, but self-centeredness expresses itself in Cain's slaying of Abel: pride in the first generation, murder in the second. The two sides of the split continue.

Men develop industry, arts, and crafts (Jabal, Jubal and Tubalcain). But evil grows apace too. ("And God saw that the wickedness of man was great in the earth and that every imagination of the thoughts of his heart was only evil continually.") The outcome of human evil in man's assertion of automony is dramatically illustrated by the story of the Tower of Babel. Men seek to build a tower to heaven, but there is no way of maintaining a corporate autonomy as against God. Each individual autonomy asserts itself against the others, and men find that they can no longer speak each other's languages. Babel becomes babble. The project fails.

To return to the Edenic myth. The story takes up the two sides of the picture separately, but in its application to real men the two sides have to be seen at once—as through a stereopticon. In the Hebrew "Adam" simply means "a man." Every man is Adam in the garden and Adam just ejected from the garden. So simultaneously: (1) we are in the image of God and are never satisfied with less than the fulfillment of our vocation, our peace depending upon our faithful creative service and fellowship; and (2) we tend to self-centeredness, tend to get in the way of others and in the way of our own true destiny. Thus true of every man at one and the same time is *imago Dei* and *peccatum originis*. The latter phrase may be confusing, but it is sound, for the dislocation is *original,* both logically and historically. As a matter of logical precedence, self-assertiveness and the desire for autonomy are at the root of all particular sins. And in the time sequence it comes first also: we are all born into a world already warped, and from the moment of our first consciousness we perceive our role in the world in a distorted way. Thus we can even vindicate the difficult text, "In sin hath my mother conceived me," if we take *in sin* to mean "into a sinful situation"— not of our own making, yet which will influence us, and which we in turn augment, to the hurt of others, by our own sinfulness.

The actual psychological and sociological fact that underlies the concept of original sin has never been portrayed better than by Archbishop William Temple:

> When we open our eyes as babies we see the world stretching out around us; we are in the middle of it; all proportions and perspectives in what we see are determined by the relation—distance, height, and so forth—of the various visible objects to ourselves. This will remain true of our bodily vision as long as we live. I am the center of the world I see; where the horizon is depends on where I stand. Now just the same thing is true at first of our mental and spiritual vision. Some things hurt us; we hope they will not happen again; we call them bad. Some things please us; we hope they will happen again; we call them good. Our standard of value is the way that things affect ourselves. So each of us takes his place in the center of his own world. But I am not the center of the world, or the standard of reference as between good and bad; I am not, and God is.*

When a wheel is not truly centered it turns eccentrically. When life is not centered on the true center of the universe it moves erratically, with disruptive results. The basis of order and unity envisioned by God in creating man is seen both in the first phase of the Garden of Eden story and in the image of heaven— in other words, before and after history. Human history itself is the story of not only the goodness and interrelatedness which has come from the true centering of men's lives, but also the story of the distortions which come from manifold false centerings,

Christianity and Social Order (Penguin, 1942), pp. 37–38. Reprinted with the permission of the original publisher, S. C. M. Press.

with every possibility and permutation of what literally are the "eccentricities" of men. Men with countless variations in individual taste, talent, inclination were meant to grow together in unity because each individual, no matter how different from the others, is centered on the *same* Center. Because this pattern has not been fulfilled there has resulted the threefold separation suggested by the Edenic myth.

Sin is separation. It involves separation from God, from one's fellow man, and from one's own true self. We can never be so far gone in sin that we are not nostalgic about our own true state and the true state of the race. It is as though a memory from the racial unconscious makes us yearn for the peace and unity of the Garden. That is why men of different climes and backgrounds and degrees of goodness all have a wistful yearning for unity with something beyond themselves, no matter how hidden this yearning may be, no matter how firm their attachment to false gods. This is why the more reflective minds of all times have pushed beyond the popular gods to a single Unity beyond them.

Similarly we yearn for unity and companionship with our fellows, no matter how accustomed we may have been to be separated from them. When in a "flashback" of memory we think of a friend of our youth, with whom relationships may have deteriorated and whom we may not have even seen for many a year, there is an ache, ever so slight, which makes us wish that the relationship had not been broken and wish that it could be restored—though with life having moved on we can conceive of no particular way that such a relationship would fit into our scheme of things, with all the changes of interests and direction in the two lives over the years. And as to the third kind of separation, we are ill content within, with our false directions so little in accord with our true make-up which still yearns to fulfill the true purpose of our creation. No man is really comfortable in his self-centeredness, no matter how impervious he seems to have rendered himself to what are the signs of his threefold separation: *God's judgment, the criticism of others,* and *self-criticism.*

All the past false centerings in the whole history of mankind are part of the cumulative situation into which each of us was born, and in recapitulating these false centerings we are both influenced by and add to this total picture of evil. It is in such a dimension as this that we must see the source and import of each particular sin. Thus we can see why, because of the social and personal history of each of us, and of all of us taken together, sin is not a matter of simple yea or nay to the particular temptation, nor—remembering that we are not free as to particular decisions but only free to follow the directions in which our gods lead us—is it a simple decision to be for the true God rather than false gods. St. Paul reflects the experience of all of us when he says, "There is another law in my members that wars with the law in my mind, and those things that I would do I do not do and those things that I would not do I do."

Such involvement would not be such a burden to us if we did not feel responsible for the actual results of it. As we have seen, we *do* feel responsible for our particular actions, despite the complications of influences, from within and without, which bear upon the particular decisions reached. The inescapable fact is that *we* are the subjects of which our given malfeasances, misfeasances and nonfeasances are *predicated;* thus "the memory of them is grievous unto us, the burden of them is intolerable." Various defense mechanisms and rationalizations which we will discuss in the next chapter may have succeeded with particular individuals in making this statement untrue as far as the conscious level is concerned, but even with them it is generally true on the unconscious level, as psychoanalysis usually discloses.

However, the actual burden of guilt is greater than the one we generally recognize. Our social involvement in sin does not mean only that social influences for which we are not responsible have influenced us toward self-centered behavior, nor only that our individual sins further the sinful influence of the body politic. In addition, each of us is jointly and positively responsible for the evil conditions in the world. I may be against war, but I am a member of mankind which wars; more particularly I am a citizen of a nation which has contributed and does contribute its own corporate self-assertiveness and its failure to effectuate its good intentions, to the disquietude of the world. And I may reap benefits from a world war which I could not alone have created and which I may well wish were not going on. Even if my nation or if I personally had decided that the conduct of the war was the lesser of two evils, it is nevertheless an evil. And, as in the case of the last war, the economy prospered because of wartime industry and most people's incomes were higher because of the war: so people fatten on evil.

Likewise with a social evil like segregation and discrimination. I may be personally opposed to these things, but my own status in society is enhanced by the fact that I am a member of the white race. I may find myself, in certain parts of the country, favored by the advantages which rest upon the evil fact of differential treatment based on race. It is not enough to say, "I can't do anything about it." In the light of the challenge to serve God with full strength and neighbor as self, I probably do not do all that I could to meet such a claim—a claim which I can only, by moral myopia, limit to individual relationships. To say that the individual is not responsible for these things, but only the nation or the culture, is really to say that nobody is responsible and that there is no such thing as wrong or guilt beyond the single acts of individuals or the joint action of well-defined groups of conspirators. To deny this problem is to say that public, national, and international life is a moral jungle free from the realm of human responsibility, or to say that social evils are merely the responsibility of those who hold office—as if we have no responsibility for the latter—a position particularly false in democracy and in a measure so even under a tyranny (there being under certain circumstances an obligation to revolt).

When we take into account the sum total, in our individual areas of vocation, of failure to keep the law of love, and of our part in the distortions of the social structure which hurt sons of men, we will feel the force of the word in the First Epistle of John, "If we say we have no sin, we deceive ourselves and the truth is not in us." Then we can respond to the candor of, "We have left undone those things which we ought to have done; and we have done those things which we ought not to have done; and there is no health in us."

Realism would seem to require such an analysis. Yet it is possible so to underline the sinful inclinations of man and his involvement in corporate sin that one is driven to throw up his hands and say, "I can't help it." Here we must remember the other side of man's nature. All of us have had the experience, in spite of the strongest temptations and influences to the contrary, of doing positively good things, things quite out of line with the whole social milieu. And in so doing we recognized the attachment of the self to good and the natural joy of attaining it. This joy is matched by a sense of guilt when we do not do good—no matter how we may explain our failures or mitigate our blame by reciting the attendant personal and social factors. And when we do do good and resist temptation, we find our happiness not so much in the fact of having done a good thing, with a good motive, but in the evidence it affords that to that measure at least we have been *for* the right things. We may even have perceived ourselves as on God's side in the perennial conflict of good and evil. The best argument against a view of "depravity" which sees man as utterly bereft of goodness is the repeated experience of—to use a Sunday-school phrase—"doing the hard right instead of the easy wrong."

People have stood loyally by their marriage vows in spite of enforced separation and the temptations of nature and attractive companionships; men have given sacrificially of their substance to meet the pressing needs of others; men have told the truth

C*

when to lie would have been much more convenient or safer. People do these things because of what they *are,* and what they are is determined by what they put first in life, that is, what they worship.

Men with low standards feel uncomfortable in the presence of such goodness. That is why they prefer to belittle or even debunk the goodness of others rather than to recognize it openly as a challenge to their own conduct and, beyond that, to what they are and to what they stand for. For the good things men do are constant reminders of the guilt attached to evil-doing. This is not simply that Brown's goodness is a judgment on Black's evil-doing. Brown's goodness in some particulars is a judgment on Brown's evil-doing in other particulars. Good deeds are the token of the good life that we know we are called to lead. And thus they stand as angels of judgment on the unconverted, ill-dedicated parts of our character and personality. The reality of goodness is the best proof of the reality of sin, and the good conscience that goes with right doing is congruent with the sense of guilt that goes with sin. Taken together, they are the reminders of the dual nature of man: *imago Dei* and *peccatum originis.*

CHAPTER VII

Beyond Sin: Justification

It would seem that now we should proceed to spell out the meaning of goodness and of sin in the various aspects of personal and social life. But consideration of the general principles of ethics which simply ends with the gravity of sin hardly supplies us with courage to go on and explicate the norms as to particular fields. The reason why Christianity has had the courage to proclaim God's total claim on life—the continuing divine judgment on human behavior in which motive as well as external act is brought to account, and to extend this vocation, law and judgment to every realm of human activity— is that all along in the process there has been a confidence in something beyond sin, a realization that God is more than judge. In fact, one of the principal ways—both in the most profound Christian thought and in grass-roots evangelistic preaching—for impressing men with the reality and gravity of sin has been to lay the foundation for an appreciation of the activity of God as Saviour. An Augustine, who knew the seriousness of his sins, could cry, *"O felix culpa!* O happy guilt that brought so great a redemption." And this has been the experience of thousands before and after his time. It was St. Paul's recognition of the law in his members that warred with the law in his mind that caused him to go on and ask the question, "Who will deliver me from the body of this death?" Consistently enough, a man who has sufficiently hardened himself against self-criticism and the criticism of others that he thinks he is "all right"—the type to which we have referred who avers that he simply "lives by the Golden Rule"—sees no relevance in what is the keystone of the Christian religion and has never allowed God to work in his life as Redeemer. A man who thinks he is well will not go to a physician.

On the other hand, our knowledge that a physician has cures at his disposal gives us the confidence to undergo a thoroughgoing examination. Prescription furnishes a motive for diagnosis. Thus the all-out character of Christian ethics can be explained only because the *law* is not the last word in the Christian religion. And, entirely apart from theory, an individual is not likely to accept the full dimension of the ethics unless he has confidence that there are resources beyond the ethics. All men seek some basis of self-acceptance. If they do not know a way beyond ethics they will seek to accept themselves within ethics—by the process of lowering the ethical standard to fit their own measure or by the use of rationalizations to enable them to find bad to be good or otherwise to render themselves blameless and hence acceptable to themselves.

There is a second consideration which takes us back to theology before we can proceed with ethics. We are concerned with ethics for human beings who are both free and rational, not merely with rules of conduct for animals. Hence more basic than what the particular rules are is the *reason* for goodness, the motivation for ethical behavior. In one sense it is enough to support good behavior that God has required such behavior. But since, as we have seen, our relationship with God is personal, not abstract, what kind of a person He is and how He has related himself to us determines the extent of our attraction to goodness and the character of our motivation to goodness. An especially fruitful motive for any action in interpersonal relations is *gratitude*. We naturally desire to express our thanks for what is given us beyond our merits. Again, a man who thinks that his own merits are enough will lack the motivation of gratitude for God's dealing with us in our sins. For the Stoic the motivation for goodness is that the world is structured on the basis of goodness. This is a sound motive, but it does not approach the fullness and warmth of the Christian's motivation. The Christian also wants to be good because God has taken pain to enter into the hurt and guilt of his sins and has redeemed him from them.

And there is a third consideration which calls for an entry into the field of theology at this point in our analysis. After he has broken the back of a disease a good physician guides his patient in ways which will bring him to an increasingly better health. So for the Christian, God not only supplies diagnosis of the illness (the work of judgment), not only saves the patient (the work of redemption); He has given us His Holy Spirit to channelize the motive of gratitude into increasing fulfillment of our vocation. This is the work of sanctification. Thus it is that God's nature as Trinity of Father, Son, and Holy Spirit is not merely an abstract matter of the theological analysis of the nature of God; it is the full dimension of God's dealing with us. It is the theme underlying the variations of individual fulfillment. It is the structure which supports the possibility of man's whole ethical experience, a possibility which Søren Kierkegaard has summed up as "the profound humiliation of man, the boundless love of God, and endless striving born of gratitude." This is the Christian dynamic for goodness.

Perhaps the central problem of human personality is *how to reconcile self-criticism and self-acceptance*. Both are essential, yet they seem to contradict each other. The simple fact is that if a man judges himself rigorously by the whole law of love he will find himself unacceptable and yet it is essential that he find himself acceptable. This is basic both to his well-being and to his effectiveness in fulfilling his vocation. Some men achieve a high degree of self-criticism at the expense of self-acceptance; others achieve a high degree of self-acceptance at the expense of self-criticism. How can a man have a maximum of both at the same time? Since this is obviously the *desideratum* we should say at the outset that Christianity unequivocally has the answer to this problem, and, as we shall see, the answer is its unique message. This message is the core of its Gospel. But first, better to understand the centrality of the problem and the nature of man's response to Christian ethic, let us consider the various "short cuts" which have become customary among men, even Christian men, in their search for self-acceptance.

1. *Reducing the claim.* Since guilt is the measure between the "ought" and the "is" one way to relieve the sense of guilt is to lower the "ought" level to approximate the "is" level. The most common form of this has already been adverted to: stating the moral law as the Golden Rule and then conceiving of this rule in hazy terms equivalent more or less to the level of normal decency which the adherent thinks he attains. This ethical system can be summed up somewhat as follows: Mean no harm to anyone and do none (except when one simply *has* to); respect the ordinary rules of courtesy and propriety; contribute something to charity; do a good deed in the case of obvious need (but don't pamper people; you might destroy their initiative); be loyal to nation, city, and family. There are, of course, many variations on this ethical pattern.

Another way to reduce the claim is to exclude certain areas from its application. The most obvious use of this practice is by the American lay Christian who would exclude political and economic issues from religious and ethical concern. And sometimes members of another race are viewed as beyond the pale of "doing unto others what you would have them do unto you."

A third way is more or less to recognize an over-all claim but to assume that "50 per cent is passing." Many operate on the basis of a sort of unanalyzed assumption that if a man's good deeds exceed his sins he is "doing all right."

A fourth way is to assume that good intentions and resolutions about reform make everything right to date. (This is particularly convincing, because a "firm purpose of amendment" is in fact part of what we will find is the true solution.) In this matter of an escape from a sense of guilt by resolutions as to the future, the guilt feelings themselves often serve as an instrument for restoring a sense of self-acceptance. A man can, by meditation upon the evil and unworthiness of a particular past act or series of acts, emphasize his disassociation from them and feel that by his very recognition of their wrongfulness he is entirely apart from them. Though the *deed* was wrong, *he* who was the actor in the past deed now finds himself "above" it and thus denies that it is in fact a part of what he is. Particularly is this process of thought (and rationalization) indulged in in the case of illicit sexual relationships, where it is generally associated with a judgmental rejection of the partner therein— in itself another expression of self-centeredness and thus of sin.

Another rationalization associated with the technique of letting the future suffice for the past is the assumption that one's good deed tomorrow will make up for one's bad deeds yesterday. But the fact is that if one is good tomorrow one has barely kept the law: there is, as we have seen, no room for "supererogation." Naturally it is a good thing to stop sinning, but when a total lifetime claim is involved, reform does not dispose of the guilt for sins already committed.

A fifth and more thoroughgoing way of undermining the moral claim is reserved for the sophisticated. Impressed by the anthropological data as to variation in ethical codes throughout history and under different religious systems and by the sociological data as to the wide divergence in conformity to customary American mores (for example, in the realm of sexual behavior), some conclude that all moral standards are purely relative, a matter of custom or taste. This conclusion would seem to dissolve the problem of guilt entirely once and for all. (There is confusion here because of the fact that in a mature Christian ethical system we also see the relativity of codes, but in the case of the latter system the higher and absolute claim is seen to lie behind the codes.) Such people view what others call "sin" as merely maladjustment—either an unwise independence from, or overweening conformity to, established patterns.

2. *Rationalization as to particular acts.* Except for the last group, who have eliminated the possibility of fault, the reduction of the claim does not purport to dispose entirely of the problem of guilt. Even with a conventional or lax moral standard replacing the Christian one there are times when men are confronted with actions or omissions which fall below even these standards and disturb them with a sense of wrongdoing. Here our minds prove to be fertile sources of rationalization. Particularly available is the assertion, "I couldn't help it." Interestingly enough, this is a half-truth, because, as we have seen, we cannot help what we do when it comes to particular decisions. But a person using this excuse rarely traces out the full implications of his helplessness in the premises and sees that it is a judgment on his whole past and a revelation that his gods have feet of clay. A drunken driver cannot help the accident, but he is held responsible because he freely got himself into the condition he is in.

If a particular failing recurs frequently enough then we tend to generalize our helplessness into, "Well, I have my faults; who doesn't?" And the man feels comfortable in the assumption that everybody is entitled to a fault or two and does not see himself judged for that which has become a more or less permanent part of his character. Yet it is in just such persistent traits that judgment is especially seen. Here are revealed more dramatically than in individual facts just what a man's gods are.

Another common rationalization is the focusing of attention

on some good which appears to have come out of the evil. Sometimes a logical connection is found between the evil deed and the good outcome, and sometimes there is none. An example of the first: "It is probably a good thing it happened; taught me a lesson." Another example of good viewed as logically flowing from evil: A display of anger—back of which there is an accumulation of resentments, some unrelated to the object of the anger—is visited upon an employee. Though recognizing the inordinate character of the outburst, the actor concludes that it will do the object thereof "a world of good." It may indeed—perhaps it will even inspire him to get a better job elsewhere—but under the most generous interpretation it may be true that it will jolt the employee into a more self-critical view of his present task. However, what the actor conveniently overlooks in each example is that this result is an afterthought; at the time his motive represented a failure of vocation in his duty to his neighbor. As to the second situation (no rational connection), the fact is that every act in relation to others changes the "timing" of things, so that by fortuity problems and opportunities take a different shape for all involved. If A had not detained B to gossip viciously about C they would not have had the chance meeting with D which gave their business the opportunity of a lifetime. Thus the harm to C becomes "swamped" in A's mind as he thinks of the eventual outcome, though C is still a person and harm has been done to him.

No person uses any of these devices as a conscious pattern or limits himself to any one of them. In his daily search for self-acceptance a man uses one or another or combinations of these ways of thought and adds quite original ones of his own. But before summarizing our criticism of these rationalizations it is important to appreciate their significance. They certainly do establish *how essential it is to a man to be able to accept himself*. The fact that men take the time and trouble to go through such mental gymnastics rather than simply face the fact of guilt

proves that self-acceptance is essential to happiness and equilibrium. It also suggests that any religio-ethical system has failed
which cannot provide an adequate basis for meeting such a
pervasive human need.

But these short cuts are not the right way to meet the need,
for three reasons:

First, they are logically untenable. Except in the case of the
most obvious examples the reasons for this have already been
suggested.

Second, whatever they may achieve by way of a conscious
self-acceptance, they impair the capacity for self-criticism. The
persistent use of such devices keeps us in the same moral ruts.
A man who is convinced he is right all the time is in no mood
to do anything about his wrongdoing, or to change his habits,
or to take positive steps to protect himself against perennial
temptations. Thus we see the same uncritical reactions, time and
time again, to the same situations or to similar situations. People
keep on offending others in the same way and continue in the
circumscription of their vocational fulfillment. Actually one
of man's most precious qualities, the capacity for self-trans-
cendence, is surrendered by default. When "I am what I am"
becomes the norm of life then man has lost one of his distinctive
differences from the animals and the minerals.

Third, rationalization does not in fact get rid of a sense of
guilt. It simply puts blankets on top of it and lets it sink into the
unconscious depths. Something of what our vocation is is innate
in every man. His inner self simply does not believe the rationalization which would circumscribe a sense of his calling to goodness. The result is that in his unconscious mind there accumulates
a vast quantity and variety of suppressed guilt, which is unhealthy in the fullest sense of the word. Even without conscious
recall the suppressed guilt affects his physical well-being through
psychosomatic connections (which are being more widely understood these days than ever before but which still represent a
great mystery to us). But there is recall from time to time, in

dreams, in "flashbacks," in chance associations which the passing show evokes. In spite of the hyperactivity by which men seek to keep the lid down on the unconscious, the tokens of the past assert themselves and we are often treated with a veritable floor-show of demons. The freshness and clarity with which past situations reassert themselves on the conscious level from time to time remind us that we have not dissolved the past by our little rationalizations. Whether we are always conscious of the fact or not, as has been pointed out, "the memory of our sins is grievous unto us, the burden of them is intolerable."

It is commonly thought that psychoanalysis is a remedy for trouble with suppressed guilt feelings. If the accumulation of covered-up guilt feelings is considerable such anxiety may have resulted that analysis may well be the only way of bringing all the demons out into the open; then some of the guilt feelings when examined consciously may dissolve away when it is discovered that there was no guilt there in the first place, but only a baseless inhibition. But as to a sense of guilt which was founded on actual guilt, the problem remains. There are two alternatives, and these sum up the whole problem. Either the patient will muster new rationalizations and cover up the guilt feelings again, forcing them back into the unconscious, or else he will suffer loss of self-respect by retention of the sense of guilt on the conscious level.

The cost of the latter outcome (whether as a result of professional psychoanalysis or self-analysis) is a very high one. The resulting unhappiness is obvious. Reduced also is the subject's effectiveness as a person and his capacity to do good in the future. If he feels "no good," and knows no way to relieve himself of the weight of his past, his incentive to change his negative ways is reduced and his drive to do positive good is impeded. And the process of virtually "wallowing" in his past sometimes produces a strange contradiction. Along with remorse there is often—particularly in regard to sins of sex—a wistful renewal of temptation.

What is needed is a way to be honest about the past—and yet break with it. It is precisely this that the Christian Gospel offers. It is a two-sided process, involving both God and man. On God's side it is called the *Atonement.* On man's side, *justification.*

As to God's side, we lose much of the dynamic of what can operate on man's side if we oversimplify things and simply say that God forgives sin. It cannot be *simply* this on God's part if there is preserved the full force of God's justice and God's unyielding claim to our full allegiance. This is why St. Paul in the Epistle to the Romans turns first to the problem of the *justification of God* before he turns to justification of man: assuming that God forgives, the problem is how is His righteousness maintained? If 100 per cent is expected of us—and all our lives long—how can we be acceptable to Him (and thus to ourselves) if we have broken the law—once or repeatedly. It is important for the whole ethical structure that God not lower His standards, even for the ease of our consciences. With His righteousness is at stake our dignity and meaning. And at stake too is the high seriousness of our relationship with God. If I have been insulting to an acquaintance and his reply to my protestations of regret is, "Skip it, it didn't matter to me in the least," and if I think he means it, then I know that *I* don't matter to him and that my actions, one way or the other, have no meaning for him. This one thing is anchored down in Christian theology: God doesn't "skip it." To alter the analogy, when I have offended a friend who *does* care what I do, and I say that I am sorry, I know that as he forgives me he absorbs the hurt. The Christian faith proclaims that God absorbs the hurt in forgiving us, thus maintaining His justice and absolute expectancy as to our behavior and at the same time accepting us into full standing with Him. How He does this, particularly in the supreme manifestation of it in the saving passion and death of Our Lord, is more properly the subject of theology—and a difficult part of it it is; but the *fact* that He does so is one of the three great theological premises about the nature of God on which the system of Christian ethics rests. He takes up the slack between His righteousness and our actual behavior, if we repent. He takes the burden and hurt of our sins unto Himself. He closes up the gap of separation which is our sin. In the words of the familiar hymn:

> *Just as I am, thy love unknown*
> *Has broken every barrier down.*

Thus He accepts us over and over again. And on this acceptance rests our own self-acceptance. If God accepts me, who am I not to accept myself?

"Justification" does not mean *being* right; it means being *taken for* right. If man's peace of mind depends on being right, he is foredoomed to failure in its achievements or to suffer a superficial peace purchased at the price of the numbing of self-criticism and the poisoning of the unconscious levels. But if one's peace rests on being *accounted right* by God, such acceptance comes at no price; to the repentant and believing it is free —that is, "by grace."

The Christian so justified can dare to face honestly and fully his failures of vocation, his breaches in the law of love, and at the same time can maintain his *self-respect* and his *pou sto* with God. Once having so faced himself, He is through with the past, except as a guide to changed behavior in the future. Its hurt and guilt need find no place in his unconscious levels nor need it be a drag on his conscious equilibrium. This—and this alone—is the way of reconciliation between self-criticism and self-acceptance. And in and through the process arises the most wholesome motive for goodness in the future.

CHAPTER VIII

The Dynamic for Goodness: Thanksgiving

As the world judges things, the fact that good gets done is the main thing. But in God's eyes *why* a man does a thing which, objectively speaking, may be good is of greater importance. The priority of motive in Christian ethics rests on a trans-ethical premise that the living God would be related to us personally and that that personal relationship is not only the mainspring of ethical action for the Christian but that it is a *desideratum* in itself even more important than our good deeds. God wants the deeds, but even more He wants *us*.

Thus it is that the publican—a bad man—is greater in God's eyes than the Pharisee—a good man. The former "went down to his house justified" because a personal relationship with God was established when he cried, "Lord, have mercy upon me, a sinner," and God's response was forgiveness, whereas the latter was one of those who "trusted in themselves that they were righteous." Yet in terms of external deeds, the Pharisee was more righteous, by a good deal, than the publican.

There is really no necessary correlation between external act and motive. Suppose a man is seen giving a five-dollar bill to a blind beggar. Generally speaking, this would be regarded as a good deed. But his motive may represent any of the following possibilities:

1. He may wish to receive the satisfaction of being thought generous by those who stood near by.

2. He may have stolen five dollars from the blind man's cup on a previous occasion and now wishes to pay it back.

3. He may feel guilty about something and wish to relieve his sense of guilt by a generous act.

4. He may have been asked by the blind man to help him work out a more stable solution to his problems, and his answer may have been that he didn't have time for that but that he would be glad to give him five dollars.

5. He may have a natural liking for the blind man.

6. He may dislike the blind man but, moved by gratitude for all that God has done for him, he may feel that this gift would be the best use of his available funds, considering both his own needs and his other obligations.

As to those standing around, it is all the same, and to the blind man it may be all the same. But it is not all the same to God. And in terms of Christian ethics it would be better that two dollars be given with motive number 6 than that five dollars be given with any of the other motives.

Those who are inclined to think that positive results on this earth are more important than man's relationship to God perhaps may take comfort in the fact that Christianity is confident that in the long run people operating on a motive of gratitude to God will do better deeds, have better interpersonal relations. As to the contrast between motives 5 and 6, in the one case the man likes his neighbor; in the other, though perhaps he dislikes him, he *loves* him, as the second great commandment means love (as we shall see in Chapters XIII and XIV). The important thing, however, is that the man operating under the last motive conceives of himself as a partner in God's total enterprise and acts from the motivation of gratitude to God for his status. Here we must make a distinction. If he conceives of his status as a matter of his birthright in creation, and no more, there is still lacking something essential in the personal relationship to God. There is a claim upon him in those terms; but actually he has not always lived up to this claim in the past and his right to act in that status is not a matter of right but is a matter of the continual gift of God to one who has been recreant in fulfilling the obligations of his partnership.

Pride is an unattractive trait, even in the eyes of our fellow men, whether they be religious or not. Pride as to particular objective accomplishments or as to particular proven abilities is tolerable enough (often it is in fact simply an honest appreciation of the realities of the case); but pride as to virtue or moral achievement is never tolerable. This natural distinction on the part of men is a sound one and is a reflection of God's reaction to these two kinds of pride. An attitude which denies or appears to deny what is really the truth about the source of our personal capacities is in fact a slight to Him who gave these capacities and may actually interfere with the proper active use of them. Thus when a man does good because of an appreciation of his own moral caliber, or even because of the call of vocation, he is always in danger of this wrong kind of pride. A secure foundation for a combination of the proper recognition of goodness when it is good and of the right kind of humility in the doing of it, lies in the constant recognition that our total standing before God does not rest upon our own merits (which are mediocre enough when taken in the large) but in God's continued acceptance of us when we repent of our shortcomings. Other motives we may have, but only when they are cleansed, strengthened, and inspired by gratitude is the result free from pride. Thus—and only thus—our particular works are acceptable to God.

But the motive of gratitude is not merely a negative protection against pride. It actually provides a dynamic for ethical action which exceeds any other possible motive. One may do good to another person because it is his duty (such as fulfilling one's contract or putting in one's eight hours a day with a firm); but if, in addition, there is a personal relationship, particularly one renewed by a thankfulness as to continual forgiveness for shortcomings, then there is an especial zeal for good performance and particularly toward someone who does not take advantage of our weakness by imperious or arbitrary demands. If this is true as to persons who have only a partial claim upon our time, it is all the more true of the Christian ethical claim. Even with a set code of laws it is difficult enough to obey simply out of sheer moral effort. But the Christian ethic calls for so much more than this: it calls for an imaginative *ad hoc* ethic in which the needs around one are met "on the spot," often without reference to precedents or standard generalizations. A positive utterance of the right word at the right time may save the neighbor here and now; an action taken without much forethought can be a witness to God's presence in the world. What is requisite for this kind of spontaneous ethic is a constant wellspring; and an abiding sense of gratitude can provide this wellspring.

Now we turn to the basis for this gratitude which has been the hallmark of the saints and the possession of many notable and obscure. Certainly the first basis is that of our creation, which is not simply a matter of the past tense but a continuing renewal, summed up in the words of the familiar General Thanksgiving, "our creation, preservation, and all the blessings of this life." But this can so easily become abstract. "He sendeth rain on the just and the unjust" alike, and it is so much easier to reduce all of this to nature or, more piously, to God's general workings (what the Declaration of Independence calls "nature's God"). Where God's provision becomes most personal and individual is in the experience of sin and guilt and God's acceptance of us in our sins when we have repented them and trust in His saving grace. Thus it is that the General Thanksgiving continues, "but above all for thine inestimable love in the redemption of the world by our Lord Jesus Christ; for the means of grace, and for the hope of glory." Here we find a distinctly Christian motivation for ethics. God has been good to us though we were not good, though we were not worthy, though we were not attractive. Thus we see immediately that this motive shapes the nature of our response, a response which God would have us direct toward others. We are not to be good to others just because they are good, or worthy, or attractive. We are called to be good to others because they are in need of our love and service. In our redemption God takes up the slack between Himself and us; so we are called to take up the slack between ourselves and others, to meet them in their need and not on the basis of their merits.

Thus we share in God's redemptive work in the world. As we have been called to be co-creators with Him, we are also called to be co-redeemers. We too are called to take up the hurts of the world. For this task we have been made in the image of God; for this task the Christian has been supplied the motive by the fact that through Jesus Christ God redeems him. "Beloved, if God so loved us; we ought also to love one another." (I John 4:11.)

The process by which our grateful response is channeled is called *sanctification*. As we have seen, spontaneous response to need forms an important part in the action of grateful response. But equally important is the process by which the redirection of our lives expresses itself in development of the habit of good rather than evil response in all aspects of life, including the standard, more or less codified situations. In eliminating our bad habits and getting ourselves out of the ruts of past patterns of behavior we are really following in our lives more and more the full implications of a conversion by which God has replaced one or more false gods. And in this process we meet God again. As Holy Spirit He nourishes, inspires, and guides us. Thus the Trinitarian pattern is complete. As Father God creates us and calls us into His service. We fail to live up to His claim and in His Son He meets us in our sins and restores our standing with God. In His Holy Spirit He guides us in our grateful response. Just as He is one God throughout these activities on our behalf, the Christian is meant to be *one* throughout. Rarely does his life have separate phases in which he judges his failings of vocation, experiences justification, and strives for sanctification. Actually all three processes are going on at the same time. Daily he is being judged and judging himself. Daily he is turning to God in repentance and the experience of acceptance. Daily is he seeking new levels for the fulfillment of his vocation. The turning of this wheel around and around is the dynamic of the Christian life, pushing it forward into greater fulfillment of the will of God.

We see here that, while our good works do not save us or earn us standing with God, they do figure in the picture at two points. We can never do more than God requires and we frequently do less; hence it can never be on our merits but by God's free gift—grace—that we are saved. But works are not as unimportant as some distortions of Christianity have assumed: good works are required by the law and God's measure of them is the judgment which makes us feel our need of redemption. Then our response to this free gift is a renewed striving to do good works—works which again we judge—and the cycle begins all over again. And though works are not the means of salvation they are signs by which we may know the reality of our repentance and justification. Truly, "By their fruits you shall know them," as our Lord said; and, contrary to what Luther thought, there is no real conflict between the Epistle of James, with its emphasis on works, and the teaching of St. Paul, with its emphasis on grace and faith. Faith without works *is* dead. If the promotion of goodness, or at least the delimitation of evil, does not come out of a supposed experience of justification, one can well doubt the reality of the whole experience or of one of its component parts—the repentance, the trust in God's forgiveness, or the firm purpose of amendment. St. Paul also exhorts us to do good works in every field of life. He is more precise about the relationship of these works to the full experience of the Christian life. His is a *therefore* ethic: since Christ has saved us, let us therefore behave in such a fashion. If we have really transferred our allegiance from false gods to the true God, inevitably we will do the works of the true God. Then we will have experienced the fullness of the process defined by St. Paul: "Justification by grace through faith unto good works."

Thus the ambiguity in the performance of Christians lies not in whether good works are a necessary consequence of the grace of justification but rather in the fact that for most of us our conversion is not complete. We may have turned over one or another part of our lives to God, or even the core of our being, but we have "held out" on Him as to one or more aspects of our existence. But this much can be said for a partial conversion: grace is allowed to operate in the life, and the partial convert may be inspired more and more to yield up the remaining "pockets of resistance."

We have said that sanctification is the work of the Holy Spirit. Up to now we have talked of the Holy Spirit primarily as the aspect of God which builds up community—holy esprit de corps. At the same time, He inspires the individual to transcend the community—while still of it—and be a means of judgment upon it. But in neither instance is the Holy Spirit disassociated from the life in the community. And the norms for our sanctification, paradoxically enough, have this double source. The anthropologists are right in their assumption that we learn our norms of behavior from the community in which we are raised. But they should be the last to deny that there are differences in communities. And the Christian individual, from childhood on, is informed by the ethics and mores of the *Christian* community. He never gains his ethical principles in isolation. But at the same time (and this the secular anthropologists do not sufficiently recognize) those very norms—in the case of this community at least—sometimes require him to stand apart from the ways of the community and transcend it by acts which in fact are a judgment—even upon the best of communities in the world. Men's best, even Christian men's best, is never good enough for God.

Thus the Holy Ghost speaks through those who codify and preserve the norms of the Christian community and through those who critically relate themselves to these norms. This is the work of priest and prophet we have already discussed. The phrase, "I believe in the Holy Ghost," in the Creed is followed by two characterizations after a colon: "the Holy Catholic Church" and "who spake by the prophets." Though paradoxically related, these do not represent two contradictory guides to behavior. We can see this in the fact that the revision upward by the priest of the standards of the Christian community (that is, by the official organization of the Church) has been the result always of the *avant-garde* teaching and practice of those who as prophets were "out of line." For example, a generation ago the American churches accepted segregation placidly and even regarded it as part of their convictions (as is illustrated by the official position of the Dutch Reformed Church in South Africa even today). But now there is hardly a denomination in America which has not officially labeled segregation as a sin. Practice has by no means caught up with proclamation, but the reason for the proclamation is found in the decades of prophetic denunciation and the actual practice of interracial brotherhood on the part of those who transcended the churches' current mores.

So in our individual lives. We are certainly called upon to conform to the best norms which the experience of the community has declared and lived out through the direct guidance of God, but we are also called to transcend, and in some instances contradict, these norms. The contradiction of them, if the Holy Spirit is guiding us, will be the overruling of a lower rather than a higher claim, not the relaxation of a norm in favor of a self-serving independence or a yielding to the dominance of the false god. This is the proper relationship of conformity and transcendence in the Christian life. When our Lord defended healing on the Sabbath, contrary to the norms of his day about Sabbath observance, it was because the immediate need of healing represented a more important claim upon Him than the preserving of that particular period for worship and meditation. This is a different thing from the independence of the modern churchman, by which he feels entitled to read the Sunday paper rather than go to church on Sunday morning —especially since he could just as well read the paper in the afternoon.

In making decisions, on the one hand as to the applicability to particular situations of the norms developed by the Christian community, and on the other as to occasions when we are called upon to transcend or contradict these established norms, we must rely upon the Holy Spirit, and in two important ways. These two ways are summarized in two familiar collects in the Western liturgical tradition. In the familiar Collect for Purity we pray that God will "cleanse the thoughts of our hearts by the inspiration of thy Holy Spirit" and in a familiar collect for Whitsunday we pray that the Holy Spirit will "give us a right judgment in all things" and "defend us from all error and lead us into all truth." In other words, what we are seeking is both a subjective and an objective rightness: purity of motivation and soundness of decision.

The use here of the word "rightness" may seem inconsistent with the emphasis up to this point (and in the special topics which follow) on the ambiguities involved in moral decision. When we are talking about the ethical factors in any significant human choice, realism and humility alike require us to note the evil precedents and consequents involved and to recognize the mixture of good and evil in what may be the soundest of decisions. Such recognition not only leads to greater wisdom in choice but also leads us to the need of justification and grace. Affirming the ultimacy of the claim—God as Judge—presses us toward the Cross—God as Saviour. ("I had not known sin but by the law.")

But once we know the justification which is God's gift, there is a change in the character of decision in ambiguity. "There falls, in fact, a new light over this, a light from God, and in this light everything takes on a new aspect," as Professor Søe of the University of Copenhagen tells us. What this new light reveals has never been better summarized:

It sounds inconceivably bold, and yet it is true . . . that for him who takes to himself the Gospel, God takes upon Himself responsibility for the shape the world is in—responsibility for the conditions I cannot alter, for all the past which lies fixed and unchangeable and which, precisely for this reason, is the inescapable background for my action in the present moment. I have only to look forward, hear God's claim upon me, and be obedient. All the rest becomes God's affair.

. . . I am not to let myself be crushed by the necessity which decrees that to be loving toward one must often mean failing to be loving toward another, that to undertake one task can mean having to leave other tasks untouched. That is God's affair; He must attend to that. In any case, I am given permission to turn also this burden over to Him. In faith and for faith . . . we must hold unshakeably fast to this: that in every situation there is a choice which is right and which I am permitted to make with a good conscience. I have only one thing to do: listen to God's claim and comply with it. That can be painfully difficult and have all the appearance of tragedy, as when, for the sake of a great and good cause, a man must cause other men serious sorrow. And yet, if one in faith is convinced that here lies the way of God, it is *not* tragic; for, as Professor Brunner has observed, how can it be tragic to obey God?

I know perfectly well that in the practice of life every human decision is *human*, and that means tainted with sin. But also in this we are permitted to come to God to beseech Him that He will again speak His sin-forgiving Word to this situation in the conviction that He is mighty to take into His keeping even the fateful consequences which my action may entail, take also this burden from me. The conscience which on this account is troubled I am also permitted, before *His* face, to quiet. . . .

Thus I am permitted to take existence, as it rises up to meet me in this moment, from *God's* hand, as if I had just now sprung straight from God's creative fiat. I am not to ponder painstakingly whether I am here in this situation because of my own sin or the mishandling of me by others or because of unavoidable relationships in my past life, heredity, or whatever. Rather, I am at liberty, in spite of everything, to sing God a canticle of praise for this bright day, at liberty to believe that God has created me, precisely me, that God wills me here in order that here, precisely here, I, precisely as I am, shall hear His word to me and do His will.*

*N. H. Søe, *Livets Gaade—Korsets Gaade* (Copenhagen: G. E. C. Gads Forlag, 1947), pp. 15–18. Passage suggested and translated by Canon Howard A. Johnson and used with the consent of the author.

CHAPTER IX

Worship and Evangelism

So far we have been considering the first great commandment ("Thou shalt love the Lord thy God with all thy heart, and with all thy soul, and with all thy mind") in the broad terms of vocation—the requirement that we must use all our talents and energies in the service of God in the world. However, the commandment obviously has a more direct reference; namely, to the actual worship of God. Hence this we should consider before passing on to the special obligations which fall under the general claim of vocation.

In this more direct connotation the "first and great commandment" parallels the first two of the Ten Commandments. The command to worship has two validations. The first is a direct one: Christian ethics unequivocally starts with God; thus our first ethical duty is the exaltation of God in our lives. The second is indirect; namely, as a means of supporting us in our other ethical duties. It is important that we turn first to the direct validation of the commandment lest we appear to be justifying worship merely as a means to an end less than itself.

D

Obviously, if duty to man is a high claim upon us under God, duty to God is even more primary. While, as we shall see, the fulfillment of our duty of the worship of God can actually strengthen us in the fulfillment of our duty to men and in our personal fulfillment, more important is the fact that we are bidden to worship God for His own sake, and this obligation is the primary one.

An ethic that is grounded in abstract principles needs no worship. An ethic based on the devotion of a person to a person immediately implies it. In personal relationship, such as the one between husband and wife in marriage, what either does to the other by way of individual acts or omissions is of course important, but even more important is that they maintain the relationship itself and acknowledge it before the world. Interestingly enough, in "alienation of affection" suits there is an item of damage permitted for "loss of consort." This is because the loss of the company of the spouse, though an intangible matter, is the *basic* loss. So too in our life with God. As we have already indicated, He is *at least* a person and hence capable of personal relationship with us. That He desires to be related to us personally is the basis of our dignity. While there are many things He would have us do (for each of us a very special set of things, depending on who we are and what we can do) there is one thing that He would require of us all, namely, that the basic relationship with Him be kept intact.

Worship is principally just that: keeping related on a person-to-person basis with God. Thus the Christian duty of worship is grounded in more than abstract legal demands. It is the fulfillment of our own nature at a most fundamental level. It is not simply something added by way of obligation or special benefit, over and above our regular ethical duties. From the beginning man was so made that he is not fulfilled without a personal relationship with God. We can see an analogy in the relationship of parent and child. The parent's love for the child and the child's response to it is not something added to what the child normally is; as the psychiatrists and psychoanalysts remind us, a person denied this love as a child may be actually less than a person—a crippled person. Our relationship with God is no less basic; indeed, it is more basic. The way that men give themselves headlong to various persons and objects outside themselves is simply a reflection of the fact that completeness cannot be found when a man is his own center. But the limited and contingent character of all objects or persons to whom we might give ourselves means that no such act of devotion can complete us, nor can any number of such relationships added together.

Men are constantly seeking, whether they know it or not, an abiding and secure relationship which will be full and complete, matching up with each aspect of their own beings. It is not enough, either for our own fulfillment or in terms of our loyalty to God, that we put Him first intellectually or even in terms of action. We must *know* Him Who knows us; we must consciously acknowledge to the world this relationship as the source both of our vocation and of our acceptance. This is worship.

The second validation for worship—though this is not its primary justification—is the fact that worship can be of significant support in the working out of a Christian ethical life.

Since the whole basis of Christian ethics is the claim of vocation, it is obviously of value to keep that claim before our minds through a vivid awareness of the source of the claim. Regular involvement in worship supplies us with a reliable structure for keeping conscious the basis of our lifework and of our particular decisions. Too, as to this matter of particular decisions, a continued form of objective guidance as to the various forms of the ethical activity and instruction on the principles at stake in given situations is provided by the teaching function of worship. In a sense the preaching of every sermon and the reading of every lesson of Scripture is like the firing of a blunderbuss:

there may be those who need the particular word uttered at a particular moment. On the other hand, it is fortunate that it is not possible to "tailor" the sermons and lessons to the needs of the persons present, because the seasoned experience which both the written tradition and the preaching represent is likely to throw light on particular situations in a way which neither the preacher nor the hearer might in advance have suspected was relevant. More than that, since the scene is always shifting as to this matter of decision, a life well stocked with the various insights of the corporate tradition, as inspired by God, and one constantly "refueled" over the years by a consistent process of worship, is bound to be able better to meet particular problems as they come up than one which takes counsel only on particular points as they arise.

But more far reaching than either of these considerations is the fact that in worship we re-enact the steps of the process which is the dynamic for our ethic: God's call to us, our failure to live up to our vocation, His forgiveness and acceptance of us, and our grateful response thereto.

Christian worship is of two general types: services of the Word (or "choir offices"), which are the continuation of the synagogue service, and the Eucharist (or the Lord's Supper), which is the continuation of the temple service. Each in its own way recapitulates each of man's basic relationships to God and the motivation for his ethical action.

Let us examine the constituent elements of a typical "service of the Word." First there is an acknowledgment of God's presence (the "invocation" or "opening sentences"). This is generally followed by a confession of sins (such as "the General Confession"). We quite naturally feel a sense of guilt when we are faced with the presence of God because we are reminded of our vocation to serve Him and of our failure to fulfill our vocation. The perennial psychological appropriateness of this reaction is attested by the fact that the same is recorded as the experience of Isaiah. After the great vision of God in the temple

Isaiah cries, "Woe is me! for I am undone: I am a man of unclean lips, and I dwell in the midst of a people of unclean lips. . . ."

Then follows the Absolution or assurance of forgiveness, again corresponding to the experience of Isaiah: "Then flew one of the seraphims unto me, having a live coal in his hand, which he had taken with the tongs from off the altar: and said, lo, this hath touched thy lips; and thine iniquity is taken away and thy sin purged." Thus do we say, "O Lord, open thou our lips": it is through His gift and not our merit that we are meet to praise God—now in psalm and canticle. The next step is a natural one: we want to know God's will for us and the basis of our continued dealings with Him: we listen to His Word in lessons from Scripture: "Also I heard the voice of the Lord, saying, . . ." And what He says is not merely concerned with abstract verities. It is a call to action: "Whom shall I send, and who will go for us?" And our response is the song of loyalty and pledge of allegiance (the Creed), prayer that we may be fitted to serve, and a final affirmation of the sense of thanksgiving which is our motive for action: "Then said I, here am I, send me."

So in a "service of the Word" is re-enacted the whole cycle of our life under God. Even more vividly are certain elements of the cycle portrayed in the Eucharist. After another form of a service of the Word (pro-anaphora, ante-communion, or mass of the catechumens), in which appear some of the elements considered above, there are three great acts in the drama (with the themes intertwined in some liturgies): Offertory, Consecration and Communion, Thanksgiving.

In the Offertory we present, through tokens, *ourselves and our lives*. But the Offertory does not end with the presentation of alms and oblations: we do not hold ourselves before God as a perfect offering: we are *inadequate* and *needful* (hence the great intercession, or Prayer for the Church, as in one familiar form: "We humbly beseech thee most mercifully to accept our alms and oblations, and to receive these our prayers, which we offer to thy divine majesty"), and we are *sinful* (hence the confession and Absolution or assurance).

The second theme is generally announced with the *Sursum corda* ("Lift up your hearts") and the grouping of ourselves with "the whole company of Heaven" in participation in the Divine action which is to follow. Then there is recited the historical yet eternal basis of our forgiveness and acceptance—the saving work of Christ, and there is affirmed our here-and-now identification with His sacrifice re-presented. Then, in and through the very tokens of our inadequate and sinful selves which have been offered, sanctified not by our own achievement but by His Holy Spirit working in the fellowship, His presence and grace are communicated to us. Thus is removed our alienation from God, from our neighbors, and from our true selves.

The third theme really begins as the second ends. Our reception of "these holy mysteries" is our grateful response to God's gift, and we express this new motivation in a "prayer of thanksgiving" for our fellowship with Him and with "the blessed company of all faithful people" and for the fact that we are "heirs through hope" of His "everlasting kingdom." Action springs from thanksgiving, as we pray for grace to "continue in that holy fellowship, and do all such good works as thou hast prepared for us to walk in. . . ." Our new joy in the threefold experience is set forth in a hymn of exultation (usually the traditional *Gloria in excelsis*); and, with a blessing, we set forth to the tasks of our earthly life.

Thus is corporately re-enacted the three elements which provide the dynamic for goodness: "the profound humiliation of man, the boundless love of God, the endless striving born of gratitude."

To those who say "it is better to have these things in our minds and hearts than to affirm them with our lips" the answer is yes. But to assume that what we affirm with our lips and physically involve ourselves in has no bearing on what is in our minds and hearts is to affirm a psychosomatic discorrelation that we no longer assume in either pedagogy or therapy. The answer is both/and, not either/or.

This salutory experience of worship speaks not only to the conscious mind; it can, through the well-worn channels of familiar symbol and phraseology, reach the unconscious levels as well. Just as the unconscious mind projects into our conscious levels the images of insecurity, alienation, and self-assertion, we can introject into the unconscious mind symbols of security, acceptance, and self-giving. These wholesome symbols—and the realities for which they stand—can wrestle with the demons within which seek to devour us.

If our suppressed fears, guilts, and resentments, our frustrations and sense of meaninglessness have accumulated enough force seriously to distort the functioning of the conscious personality, then psychoanalysis is called for. However, for most people this is out of the question, not only because in many instances it would do more harm than good, but also because of the practical fact that there are not enough analysts to analyze everybody anyway.

Hence the importance of the regular introjection into the unconscious levels of the symbols—and of the realities—of security, acceptance, and meaningful relationship. These of course reach the inner man more effectively if they come by way of familiar channels and if their symbolic form is such as to awaken the poetic imagination. The power of rational analysis can be overused in this experience (it can even serve as an impediment: though, to be sure, we do not want to utilize symbols which have no rational basis).

Obviously then the experience of worship serves both the purpose of cure and the purpose of prevention. The building up of a healthy inner make-up is bound to strengthen any individual against the tides of life which can be destructive to conscious and unconscious integration. Any form of worship will have an effect upon us, whether it be worship of the devil (either obtusely in the form of something like a "Black Mass" or in the disguised form of much of our modern foci of entertainment) or the most sublime adoration of the transcendent God. All of our accustomed associations and routines have an effect upon us, and in no case can we be impervious to influences upon the unconscious. The problem is one of selection and intensification. We should choose as regular experiences those which will speak to our lives the things which we believe will make for stability, courage, and joy. Obviously we should not subject ourselves to experiences which will say things which conscience and reason do not vindicate as true. But if we are convinced of the truth of a religious tradition then we should be eager to have it become part of the whole self and not merely a part of the conscious mind.

But here we are concerned with ethics, not with the prudential character of an act; and, being concerned with ethics, we are bound to carry the point one step further. *If* we regard the experience of sound worship (that is, worship adequately expressing what we conceive to be the truth about the world and ourselves) as wholesome and good, *if* it does re-enact vividly for us the whole cycle of vocation, judgment, grace, and thankful purpose of amendment, *if* it does hold before us the scope of our vocation, *if* it does remind us of the specifications of an ethical life, then this experience is more than a "good thing"; it is more than something that is "advisable"; it is an ethical duty. This argument is secondary to the basic one already stated, namely, that it is an ethical duty to worship God in order to maintain the relationship with God which lies at the foundation of any Christian ethic. But for this second reason also worship is our duty, since anything which can contribute to the fulfillment of our vocation and the living out of our Christian life is of obligation.

If a man feels called to be a lawyer, it is his duty to undergo the experience of three years of legal study. It is also his duty to continue to keep up his particular specialty which he is following, reading its literature, following the relevant decisions of the courts, entirely apart from any direct or obvious advantage or pleasure which may come from such activity. For a naval officer "refresher" courses are a regular part of his naval "duty," because such experiences will advance his supply of information and strengthen his loyalty to the service, both of which are likely to increase the effective performance of his more customary assignments. In other words, the pursuing of these courses is not an "extra," nor is it something pursued in his spare time or on leave, but rather a part of his regular service. Similarly worship is not an extra or an opportunity which we are free to take or leave. It is a regular "refresher." Over and over again the full scope of our vocation is affirmed and we are put in touch with the dynamic for the performance of the same. If we are under obligation to be good we are under an obligation to engage in supporting activities which motivate us and guide us in the way of goodness.

So far we have been thinking of the primary duties of the individual and the effect of worship upon him in the fulfillment of his duties. This ethical obligation does not merely rest on a claim that the Christian way of life is good for those who happen to hold the faith; it maintains that this way of life is good for all men. Hence our duty to other people is greater than merely doing good for them. We also have a duty to bring to them the real basis of goodness which is found in a living relationship to God. Anyone is grateful to a friend who gives him cut flowers, but we are more grateful to one who gives us seeds or bulbs: for then we can grow flowers for evermore. Hence the greatest thing we can do for another man is to impart to him that religious faith which will lift him up out of idolatrous concerns and charge him with a high sense of vocation and invite him to share in the resources of judgment, grace, and thanksgiving offered by the Christian religion.

Loyal participation in the worship of the Church is the principal means whereby we keep alive and spread in the world the religion upon which our ethic is based and which gives the re-

D*

sources for the Christian life. Generally speaking, empty churches are poor arguments for the Christian way. Hence, to put it on the most minimal basis, each of us has an ethical duty to see that there is one less vacant seat and so thus to reduce *pro tanto* the negative witness of emptiness and thus positively increase the effective proclaiming of God's presence in the world. Holding the ideas of the Christian faith or even practicing its ethic is not enough; nor is it enough simply to give to the financial support of the immediate institution. Nothing takes the place of the personal witness of regular and loyal worship. But our duty to our brothers who need the wholeness which can come from accepting the Christian understanding of life and action requires much more of us. Here we enter more obviously the field of evangelism.

The very word "evangelism" puts most people off. It suggests emotional preaching and the "Are you saved, brother?" of the midnight mission. Before discarding these obtuse examples it is well for us to recognize that, in terms of *intent,* even these types of evangelism are right. The desire to save men is entirely sound and is an ethical obligation upon all of us. But obviously some people are driven further from the claims of God by a firm hold on the lapel with one hand and the passing of a tract with the other. Obviously in the performance of this ethical duty, as in the case of any other, we are called upon to take thought to select the very best means in each individual situation. That there is a duty to bring the Christian faith and the dynamic for Christian ethics to everyone to whom we can bring it would seem to be unquestionable.

The point is labored, however,. because there are so many ostensibly loyal Christians who "do not believe in missions." Behind this type of comment usually lie two attitudes (singly or in mixture), one of them good, the other unfortunate. The first is a wholesome respect for the ideas and motifs which dominate the lives of others and a respect for their privacy and their right to organize their lives around any center which they may choose as their god or gods. The second factor is less commendable: it is that the author of the statement really takes a relativistic view toward Christian faith and ethics. He has really reduced them to the category of mores. In other words, the very quality of Christian theology is changed by the assumption that its view of the purpose of God and the structure of the universe is but a particular development within a particular culture. The truth in the proposition is that we should recognize the relativity of particular *ways* of expressing the faith or of performing the Christian ethical demand. But to assume that the faith and the demand are not the meaning of God for all mankind and for all time is to dethrone God and His Christ in the world.

The best distribution of responsibility and resources between foreign missions and the home efforts of the church, and the best distribution of personal resources between evangelism and other ends, is another question. But that the missionary endeavor has a place in our ethical concern is an obvious corollary of the call to translate our faith into concern for one's neighbor.

Evangelism, of course, includes not only foreign and home missions; that is, the corporate institutional spread of the Gospel. Included—and of equal importance—is person-to-person evangelism. The natural shyness of even the convinced Christian often evokes such reactions as, "It's much better to witness to your faith by the way you behave." Of course, good behavior is a form of witness to one's faith (just as bad behavior is a way of "letting down" one's Lord). But we are brought back to the cut flowers and bulbs. The sharing with others of the source of our good deeds and the dynamic for them is of incalculably greater value to people than the sharing of the deeds themselves. The second ground of this reticence is a feeling that talking about one's religion and one's loyalty to it is a form of insufferable pride. This is due to a confusion as to the central motif of the Christian faith. If a Christian were the "good" man, then to affirm to one's friends and acquaintances that "I am a Christian" would be conceited indeed. But since a Christian is really a man who knows that on his own he is not good, and that through Christ his sins have been forgiven, to say that one is a Christian is not a conceited statement. It is rather a humble and honest attribution to God of the credit for the good deeds which the beneficiary or observer might otherwise regard as traceable only to the actor. Thus the man who affirms his faith along with his good works is less guilty of pride than the man who shows forth good works without pointing to their true Source.

CHAPTER X

God and Caesar

The Christian knows that God comes first, but a close contender for first place—even in Christian cultures —has been the State. As far as the attitude of the State itself is concerned, in most places and in most centuries the State has regarded itself as the first claim and as the authority which permits, requires, or disallows devotion to God. So far as the Church is concerned, it has generally supported this claim of the State, provided that its particular form of the worship of God is the one permitted or required. (Quite naturally it has disallowed the claim of the State when some other form of the worship of God—or no worship thereof—has been enforced by the State.) Regardless of the view we take of this relationship—and obviously it must form a considerable part of our discussion in this chapter—it is clear that the State looms large as a claim upon the individual and requires our consideration before we turn to the claims attendant upon other groupings and relationships.

Whence its authority? There is no question about its authority as an existential matter. There is no longer any place in the world left to which the jurisdiction of some state does not extend. But it is not enough from the point of view of Christian ethics to say that one obeys the law because the policeman can compel one to. And the problem is not merely theoretical: history gives us occasion over and over again where the Christian has been confronted with conflict between the claims of the State and other claims upon him. What is at stake is the weight to be attached to the claim of the State. To put the question in another way, how much finality has the civil law for the Christian?

The Christian tradition has always regarded the civil authority as stemming from God. When St. Paul says, "Honor the King," he is not being merely prudential; he includes this injunction among a list of prime ethical duties. When the Church engages to crown a king it is not merely supplying the trappings for an impressive ceremony. When Sunday-school lessons encourage loyalty to one's country they are not merely aping the public school civics class.

Yet it is difficult on a rational basis to establish an absolute place for any particular government as an ethical claim upon the individual. The existence of particular national groupings has no abstract logic; it is merely an historical fact. That the citizens of Galveston, Texas, are subjected to the authority of Washington rather than of Mexico City is due to the fact of the Mexican War; it is not due to anything inherent in the nature of the soil of Galveston or due to any principles by which one could distinguish the people living in Galveston from those living elsewhere. We cannot ground it in "self-determination" (which meant so much to Woodrow Wilson after the First World War), since in practice we do not allow peoples this privilege, as our own Civil War illustrates. Nor can we say as a matter of abstract principle that people of the same racial, cultural, or religious backgrounds automatically constitute a governmental grouping entitled forever to a piece of territory and to the government of all living thereon. Entirely apart from the merits or demerits of Zionism, the rationale that Palestine is being *returned* to the Jews is insupportable when we realize for how many centuries it has been occupied by the Arabs and for how many centuries before the time of Moses it had been occupied by the Canaanites.

There is a further difficulty. There is actually no reality (in an ontological sense) to a nation or government beyond the particular congeries of people governing and being governed. When I obey the government I really am obeying particular individuals, whom a majority of those concerned enough to vote have elected, and their appointees. These men may or may not be the best people, or the wisest people, or the most honest people.

Then there is another consideration. Most civil obedience is not to the particular commands or directives from officials but to the scheme of laws, written and unwritten, which pertains to a particular nation. Many of these reflect commonplace ethical principles, and in our obedience to them we are simply following our consciences anyway: we do not need the government to tell us not to murder. But many of these laws are quite arbitrary from a logical point of view and have no obvious grounding in ethical principle: a man must file his income tax on April 15 and not on May 1, which as far as the heavenlies are concerned may be just as suitable a day and, so far as the needs of his personal vocation are concerned, perhaps a better day. In terms of his personal fulfillment of vocation a man's time might be put to better use, with no actual harm to his neighbors, if he parked his car in a taxicab zone where there was a reasonable expectation that no cabs would be arriving that day, rather than parking his car four blocks away and walking to a destination where he has ten minutes' business to pursue. Conformity to such a traffic regulation for fear of getting a ticket has no particular ethical quality about it. Since all of his life is under judgment, a Christian is supposed to be making his decisions on a higher basis than the fear of earthly sanctions. It is true one could reason that the time, trouble, and cost attendant upon a traffic ticket would interfere more with the optimum use of his time than the time taken in walking four blocks to and fro. But this consideration does not really cover the case when a man is very short of time today and not sure that he will be tomorrow, or when he might have a reason to believe that he may safely "gamble" on the chances of getting a ticket. Assume then that I am a "good citizen" and simply decide to obey the law without taking into account all of these other considerations; what is the ethical basis of my conformity? In other words, why, apart from force or fear, should I obey what others—who are simply men like myself—tell me to do when they speak in the name of a government—which is, of course, a transient phase of history? Is there any eternal grounding for governmental authority?

The answer is yes, and the reason is to be found in what is the foundation for all Christian ethical action, a Christian's vocation. All theories of government aside, the fact is that I can better fulfill my role as a creative, redemptive, community-building individual in an ordered society than I can in the midst of anarchy. And as for the second great commandment, I am better able to serve my neighbor and bring to him those things that I can value for myself in an ordered society than in a state of anarchy, and he in turn is better able so to serve in an ordered society. Therefore it is my duty to support the order of the State and to do my part to maintain loyalty and obedience among its citizens. St. Paul said, "Honor the King"; he did not say, "Honor the *good* King." When Christians said, "Render unto Caesar what is Caesar's," they did not add, ". . . as long as Caesar is a good emperor." This is because the Christian's obligation to the State is an obligation to that authority which brings order into society and makes possible thereby many good things of life, including spiritual fulfillment. We have seen that one of God's principal tasks has been that of bringing order out of chaos; thus whoever in the world helps achieve this is to that extent a servant of God. Jesus recognized a source of civil authority when He said to Pilate, "You would have no power over me unless it had been given you from above. . . ." (St. John 19:11.)

Thus, in recognizing the authority of the State, insofar as it does not conflict with other obligations of conscience, we recognize the authority of God. When the State provides us with good roads instead of muddy lanes, disposes of the sewage, and restrains criminals, it is doing the work of God and we can respect it for His sake.

When our allegiance to the State is thus qualified, and the derivative character of our allegiance to it is thus recognized, we are saved from political absolutism and at the same time can really render unto God that which is God's and to Caesar that which is Caesar's. Under such an analysis God and not Caesar is the final claim on conscience.

Several implications arise from this view of the matter:

1. This approach does not depend upon there being any logical basis for a particular state's being in existence. It takes a given state in a given area as a fact—however it may have arisen historically and however suitable or unsuitable its extent or structure may be, judged by purely rational grounds.

2. This approach does not rest on any particular ontological theory which gives the State a substantive or organic reality apart from the individuals who compose it and its government. The congeries which make possible enforceable commands is a fact, whatever may be their metaphysical basis in the minds of one or another of its more reflective citizens.

3. This approach gives a basis for obedience which does not rest upon or require an individual decision each time as to the balance of interests at stake. In general I know that my ability and my neighbors' ability to function is furthered by reliable—even if arbitrary—arrangements. Therefore I do not violate the law in a particular instance even though under the circumstances an individual weighing of the interests at stake might seem to justify my doing so (e.g., when it would appear to do no harm at the moment for me to park in a given place and there is considerable value to me in so doing).

4. This theory of things does not require a "divine right of

kings" or any other theory by which we conceive of the officers of the State acting for God in a way different from other people in the exercise of their vocations. If he is fulfilling a Christian vocation the official of government is of course acting for God —but in no way that is qualitatively different from what a businessman may be doing in a particular realm of activity.

5. When civil obedience is based upon vocation, then simultaneously the same basis is afforded for civil *dis*obedience in appropriate cases.

This latter consideration leads us to the most important problem in the field. Assuming that there is a basis—as above outlined—for loyalty to the State, in what circumstances may or should the Church or the individual disobey the law of the land on the ground of a higher loyalty?

Many citizens—including people who would call themselves Christians—would answer, "Under no circumstances." God will judge the evil, but it is not up to the people to do so. It is their simple ethical and religious duty to obey. But such an attitude is not limited to the days of absolute monarchy. There are many American Christians who assume that America is the main thing, that religious or ethical claims are secondary, and that if the civil law requires or forbids something it is not up to the Church or the individual to consider taking an opposite course. For example, not long ago an issue was raised as to whether a certain theological seminary in the South should admit Negro students. For a time, for many of the Christian trustees and others interested in the matter, it was enough that such admission would have been contrary to the law of the State.

Obviously such a conclusion is untenable on the premises on which we have been proceeding, for it represents the finalization of something which is a transient part of history. It is to make the State God; it is to cry, "We have no king but Caesar." When God's claim upon us is secondary to the majority of a state legislature he is no longer God.

Nor has the Christian Church at its best moments ever accepted the State with such a finality. The early Christians in the Roman Empire would not put the incense in the thurible at the emperor's shrine, though the law quite clearly required it, but went underground instead, with the consequences of martyrdom on the one hand and growth of the Church on the other. ("The blood of the martyrs is the seed of the Church.") And St. Ambrose, as Bishop of Milan, stood the emperor down at the steps of his Cathedral Church, excommunicating him for an unjustified purge of a city. Martin Luther, at the Diet of Worms, declined to follow the will of the leaders of the empire. Inspired by a religiously grounded ethical concern, citizens spirited slaves out of the South in spite of the Fugitive Slave Law and the ruling of the nation's highest adjudicatory in the *Dred Scott* decision. And in more recent times churches and other institutions have violated laws and ordinances requiring segregation, even in advance of the recent Supreme Court decisions which would seem to nullify such laws. And during the last war the underground in France, the Low Countries, and the Scandinavian countries, for example, violated on religious principle the "security regulations" of the then governments of their particular countries.

Thus we see the paradox of support by Christianity for the institution of the State and support for those who have from time to time rebelled against the authority of the State. The existence of the paradox is enough to make clear that the State is not final in any system of Christian ethics. Civil law falls in the class of ethical codes, which we have already considered in relationship to the total claim of the two great commandments which express Christian vocation. And the paradox must be resolved in much the same way. Normally it would be simpler to obey the law. This covers rather easily most decisions we have to make. Even when a considerable ethical advantage is blocked by such obedience, the value of conformity and the example of respect for the order of the State may well outweigh the given advantage.

But when the ethical issue is great enough then a higher law operates to nullify in the Christian conscience the claim of the State.

In the light of the ethical analysis we have made, several principles should be kept in mind in deciding such an issue:

1. As already suggested, the ethical issue must be a significant one, so great is the value of order and civil peace.

2. Every step possible must be taken to achieve the given ethical object without violation of the law. This includes the following possibilities:

   A. A "legal" way may be sought to preserve the ethical interests. For example, if in a given country a group other than the established Church may worship only by "registering," then by all means the group should register. Or if conscientious objection to participation in war is a recognized exception to the law, but must be applied for through regular draft machinery, then there would seem to be no reasonable excuse for not making such application in the regular way.

   B. Every effort must be made for the use of such political wisdom and co-operation as is possible to effect the repeal of the law which is in conflict with Christian conscience. And there is an analogous step in appropriate cases: where there is an ambiguity in its wording or meaning every effort should be made to procure an interpretation of the law which respects the conscientious principle involved.

   c. Either prior to or following the last step—depending upon the political possibilities—judicial action should be taken to have the law declared unconstitutional (if in the particular nation such procedure is possible). Usually to bring such a case to an issue a violation of the law will be necessary and would of course be justified.

3. If all these measures have failed, then civil disobedience may be called for.

It is at this latter point that the paradox is most clearly demonstrated in action. That God is higher than the State is exemplified by the disobedience; that the order of the State is entitled to respect and support is exemplified by willing acceptance of the punishment called for by the law. It may well be that the reaction to the arrest may strengthen the hands of those who are seeking to change the law, but while it *is* the law civil obedience in taking the punishment balances off the civil disobedience of violating the law.

This attitude has been most frequently exemplified in modern times by those whose consciences have brought them into opposition to the State over the issue of war. The occasion of such conflict is somewhat reduced where conscientious objection is made a legal exemption from military service, but even where this is the case, a problem remains for two groups: (1) those who are not adjudged eligible for the exemption but who nevertheless regard themselves as conscientiously opposed to participation in war; and (2) those who regard it as necessary to their witness against war not to register at all. The standing, in ethical terms, of these latter positions depends on a more fundamental problem: the ethics of war and peace.

That *war*—any war—is an evil needs no argument, especially these days when the price of another total war may be the obliteration of the human race. It is fruitless to talk of a "just war," since any war *reflects* existing conditions of injustice—generally on both sides—and *results* in grave injustices, whoever wins. Hence the first ethical duty of all men—a duty heavier in proportion to a man's degree of influence—is to work for the prevention of war. This is not merely a negative duty—to abstain from jingoism; it is a positive duty to promote peace, to support efforts toward just and peaceable solutions of international issues, and to further those agencies of international consultation and co-operation which give promise of increasingly attaining these ends. Thus for Christian men in our day interest in and support of the United Nations cannot be a mere hobby of a few; it is a claim on all—each to the measure of his own capacity.

On this pacifists and non-pacifists can agree (though many in each group may well have been failing to act accordingly). And increasingly, with the development of nuclear weapons, we can expect them to agree in the resultant opinion, if not in the supporting analysis, regarding aggressive war. There may have been a day when to right some grave wrong an aggressive war was called for (though there has generally been a mixture of motives: the Spanish-American War is an example). But today counterbalancing any possible goodness which could be achieved by aggressive action is not only the loss of x number of lives (serious enough in any case) but also the likely destruction of the possibility of civilized life on our planet. With this the truth of the matter, it is impossible to conceive of a state of affairs in which it could be reasonably concluded that a war was the best solution. The evil to be remedied would have to be gross beyond imagination to justify a repetition—on a terrestrial scale—of Samson in Gaza.

But suppose another nation starts an aggressive war. What then? Here the pacifist and non-pacifist divide. The pacifist takes a direct line, satisfying in its simplicity. Wounding and killing is wrong; we do not take part in it, even when we are attacked. But there are several difficulties with this apparently "more Christian" approach.

First, the pacifist has chosen something that is not a live option. He has chosen peace. But peace is not one of the available possibilities. The only alternatives are war with a victory by the aggressor and war with a victory by the attacked nation. A choice between the latter possibilities is not, for the Christian, an automatic one, but at least it represents the real choice.

Second, the pacifist cannot in fact disengage himself from the fact of war. Because a good many citizens feel differently than he does, and bear the brunt of the realistic situation, he may well by their military success be protected in the possession of his property. Especially if the conflict is between an authoritarian and a free nation, he is protected by the victory of the latter in his right to continue to hold his particular views. To return to his material situation, the very fact that his country is at war may mean that his investments earn more. He is not to be faulted for that as such, but all in all it is clear that he is not able to regard himself as apart from the ambiguity of good and evil which the actual situation represents. This involvement carries with it responsibility—for support of the best available good or opposition to the most menacing evil.

This responsibility is not discharged, on the other hand, by an assumption that one simply goes to war for one's country. One's final allegiance is to the heavenly country and to the earthly scene only in terms of the opportunity it provides for fulfillment, here and now, of the ends of the eternal kingdom. Freedom is better to those ends than tyranny, earthly justice better than earthly injustice; and hence the Christian must choose in each war which side's victory is most likely to provide the best chance for the success of the Kingdom of God on earth. In case of real doubt he can legitimately decide for the defense of his property, his family, and the larger family of the nation which has given him the gift of citizenship and thus protected his place on the earth. But these considerations can never be the final ones.

But even if a man on this basis decides his nation is wrong in the war he is not left in the negative position of pacifism. He is called upon to be a traitor (as the world views things) in his loyalty to a country beyond all earthly forms, a loyalty which may express itself in aid to the cause of "the enemy." We do not naturally commend this attitude when our own country is involved, because of the long-standing instruction we have had that our country has been always right in every war (though when this general conclusion is drawn little mention is made of the imperialism of the Mexican War). But we welcome the attitude readily enough when displayed by citizens of enemy countries who have risked their lives in underground efforts in the cause of freedom, which cause we represented in World Wars I and II and in the Korean and Indo-Chinese wars.

Thus the Christian is put in the position of a selective and active pacifism rather than a general and passive pacifism. The latter attitude is generally exempt from prosecution; but the former is, by the law of every land, denominated treason.

Christians have often enough in the history of the Church displayed the independence which the possibility of treason implies, but we cannot discuss this approach as idle theory. The fact that most Christians have supported the wars of their respective nations, even when in the light of historic perspective we may view the position of many of these nations as the wrong one, is a reminder of *the finiteness of human vision* (e.g., Americans at the time of the Mexican War did not know as much about its rights and wrongs as we do now) and of *the pervasiveness of original sin,* here reflected in the easy identification of the interest of one's own people with the interest of God.

Yet all the while the absolute pacifist serves an important function. He witnesses to the ultimate value of peace and the ultimate evil of war. He exercises a special vocation in this witness, though he may not always have the grace to see that his vocation is *special, not higher,* since he and his interests are affected by the actual outcome and if his nation is victorious he benefits thereby. Pacifism is a role to be fulfilled in humility—the same humility that is called for by the soldier who says the General Confession as he loads his rifle.

The suggestion that active resistance to the aims of one's nation may be called for where one conscientiously sees his nation on the wrong—or more wrong—side suggests that the man who decides for civil disobedience may not always decide passively to accept punishment as a witness to the value of the civil law of his nation. In general, as we have suggested, the conscientious dissident as to a particular law must try to witness both to his transcendent position and to the positive values of the continuing State. But to this principle there is an exception which leads to a broader problem. There are, of course, circumstances in which resistance is called for. If, in the balance between the value of maintaining civil order and respect for the State and the value of witnessing to a particular issue, the issue is so great that the former value weighs very much less—in other words, if the issue is so plenary that revolution is called for—then forcible resistance to arrest on an organized "conspiracy" basis may be called for by the Christian conscience. This is, of course, the way our nation got started (though the organized descendants of this revolution are not always to be found on the side of dissidence).

When may a Christian so interpret his vocation as to justify the support of revolution? Obviously the momentum behind revolution stems from a total complex of factors which are not easily subject to rational analysis, and we are assuming a somewhat ideal situation: a Christian deciding thoughtfully and prayerfully whether he shall join his efforts with the revolutionaries or not. Assuming the situation (which is by no means totally unrealistic), the process is the same as is involved in many other ethical choices: the weighing of goods and evils. Obviously the disruption of the established order with the consequence of turmoil and the unpredictable evils that always arise out of a new order are generally likely to be so great that the issue must be a grave one indeed to justify even a serious consideration of organized rebellion. In a democracy, where there is the opportunity for the use of more peaceable means, the possibility that the Christian conscience could justify rebellion is fairly remote. But where the very instruments of orderly protest have been denied, and where evil has entrenched itself and has gained control of the usual organs through which a protest could be registered (either sooner or later), then conspiracy toward a rebellion is not only permissible but might well be required for fulfillment of Christian vocation. But here, as in everything, a careful searching of motivation is called for: not only the discerning of *good* reasons but of the *real* reasons that supply the emotional fuel for the effort.

When the occasion is ripe, and the cause clearly just, the demonstration of revolutionary spirit on the part of Christians and the attendant sacrifices, even unto death, serve a purpose of God other than the righting of wrong. This too is a witness of God's presence in the world. It is a witness to His ultimacy as against the pretensions of any other authority. The influence of the martyrs survives generation after generation, long after they have seen their earthly days. This too is evangelism. And that it is true worship of the Almighty is recognized by the fact that Christian tradition recognizes that baptism by blood may be as efficacious as baptism by water.

The same is true as to the paradox of civil disobedience as a drastic action of protest *within* the framework of the existing governmental structure. God is eager for righteousness, and such efforts toward righteousness are worthy toward that end; but they also are a witness to the fact that Christians are to be in the world but not of it, that Christians are never to be at ease in Zion. This too is evangelism. The experience of recent years has shown that the courageous witness of the Church and of Christian people, under many varying conditions, to a loyalty higher than the State has won the attention of secular-minded and indifferent people and has been the means of the conversion of many. An uncritical conformity to existing order is a case of the salt having lost its savor. Not only is righteousness not thus advanced; neither is the cause of God in the world in its ultimate terms—the drawing of men toward God as the central allegiance in communion with their fellows similarly motivated. When the opinions of the Christian and the attitudes of the Church are merely a reflection of the conventional emotions of the society in which the Church lives and works, then obviously the Church will not commend itself to men as the means of salvation of our common life nor represent anything that can lead beyond things of earth.

CHAPTER XI

The Christian and Public Questions

Having considered the ultimate possibility required of the Christian conscience—namely, civil disobedience or even the support of revolution—let us turn to the more commonplace situation: the decision a Christian is called upon to make in reference to particular political, social, and economic issues. Here we have an opportunity to apply general principles considered in earlier chapters, especially the problem of ethical decision where there are not black-and-white choices. It is particularly obvious in this realm that one rarely has the opportunity to choose between absolute good and absolute evil: the choice is almost always between varying shades of gray in the effort to achieve positive good and to limit the evil in the world.

Let us take as an example the matter of public housing. The naïve response of the liberal might be: it is better to have people in better houses; the more housing the better; hence let us have more public housing. The naïve response of the conservative is: it is better to have things done by private enterprise; let us have no intrusion of the government into business. While both have part of the truth on their sides, the situation is actually more complicated than this. The conscientious Christian should be one who is sufficiently detached from commitments to any earthly interest or principle, so that he can evaluate in a way which will in fact leave him in the uncomfortable position of not seeing answers as clear-cut as do those people who decline to make such objective evaluation and who simply decide things upon notions which they assume are final, without critical examination, and for interests which they automatically seek to serve because they are their own interests.

To continue with our example, on the *yes* side of such an issue are the following favorable factors:

1. It certainly is the will of God that sons of men live in a reasonable degree of comfort, cleanliness, and attractiveness.

2. This is not simply the problem of the particular family; it is a problem of all of us. Under the law of love we are called upon to seek to serve each other's interest.

3. Private enterprise has not in fact provided enough housing, nor is it eager to proceed to do so in the case of low-cost housing, likely to bring a very small return if indeed not a loss.

4. In short, without public aid of some sort, many people are going to continue to live in slums—which most certainly is not in accordance with the will of God.

On the *no* side there are such factors as these:

1. Individual or voluntarily co-operative sponsorship is generally the most desirable, both in terms of what it does for the sponsors and in terms of the quality of the result, due to the imaginativeness and zeal which individual responsibility—and, since the Fall of Man, hope of personal gain—indubitably stirs.

2. Increase in public ownership increases the amount of power in the hands of government and extends "bureaucracy."

3. Because of original sin increase of such power means increase in the temptation to fraud and favoritism.

An analysis of considerations of this type should not result only in indecision. Indecision means that in effect we are counted on the side of the most vocal and effective pressure groups, and hence is a decision. What we are called to do in this field and in every other is to choose the all-round best alternative (albeit a *mixed* good) and then give it our full support so that we give our weight to the advance—at least in a measure—of goodness in the world. However, the value of the recognition of the pros and cons and of the fallible nature of any decision we reach is that, in choosing the lesser of two evils, we are at the same time moved to provide as many safeguards as we can against the evil involved in the side chosen, or that perhaps we are driven to find some adequate *tertium quid*. For example, in the instance used for illustration, should we decide to back public housing we might want a provision requiring more careful auditing of expenditures, or board or commission action rather than individual action in regard to large sums of money; or we may decide to push for larger public aid for privately sponsored low-cost housing—in other words, for subsidy rather than for direct governmental construction and ownership.

Of course very few individuals are in a position to bring about any of these measures acting individually. Therefore, a Christian may feel it his duty to associate with others who are like-minded in a particular concern and with them develop the policy which jointly they may push with proper means of propaganda. But any such corporate action raises the possibility that one of the participants may in conscience prefer a somewhat different solution than the one being pushed by the group. In this case he has an additional moral choice: supporting a proposal somewhat less acceptable to him than one of his own devising, or "bolting" the group. He may well decide to do the former—again on the basis of the greater of goods and the

lesser of evils. If there is a good chance of getting through a proposal he approves of less than one which there is very little
chance of getting through, the proper ethical decision may well
be to support the former. If Christian ethics required us to support only those proposals which we believe to represent the complete will of God for society, we would end up being thoroughly
ineffective in this fallen world.

The same considerations obviously apply in the matter of
candidates for office. God has not seen fit to send angels to
earth as candidates for office, and hence we are rarely given
the opportunity of black-and-white decisions in this realm of
the choice of those who are to govern us. So we are called
upon to make our decisions as best we can, with both purity
of heart and careful rational analysis (here, as in other realms,
we are called upon to serve God with "our whole minds"),
and then give our full support to the choice made, that there
will be the maximum possibility of its effectuation. Here again,
for any effectiveness at all, we are called upon to "go along"
with others—at the price of compromise on some matters and
some candidates.

The periodic rise of "third parties" in American life sym-
bolizes the tension involved. It has seemed to some that neither
party adequately stood for the principles which they felt they
should follow in conscience; hence they lent their support to
an independent movement. However, the regular defeat of third
parties reminds us that others may, with equal conscientiousness,
have decided to compromise and work within one of the established parties in order that their aspirations may have any
relevance at all.

Compromise? Yes, from an objective standpoint; but for the
person honestly deciding, No. As we have seen, in the midst of
moral ambiguities and for the man conscious of his sin and that
of the world—and repentant and living through grace—*the best
possible decision is the right decision, is the commanded decision.*

People, in this country especially, have been accustomed to associate themselves with pressure groups as to particular issues which seem to call for reform. This, in fact, has been a characteristic feature of the working of American democracy and one that is wholesome indeed, because it combines the ethical values of freedom and of realistic effectiveness for better conditions. The undermining of this level of corporate action in recent times through the highlighting of "guilt by association" and what we may call "guilt by mutual object" as doctrines of what will probably become a permanent word in American history—"McCarthyism"—raises a new ethical question. One must now, unfortunately—as never before—weigh against the value of co-operative effort on an important issue the risk of being "smeared," for fear that it may turn out that one or another of those associated for the same object has ties which can be called "Communist" or "Communist-front." This is not simply a selfish concern; the question bears upon one's future effectiveness in the service of God. If by a particular exercise of one's heretofore-recognized American "freedom of association" one exposes himself to the possibility of such a smear, it well may be that he is *through* as an effective force. No longer will he be listened to on any subject. An obvious solution would be to join only those groups whose membership is impeccable, but few of us have investigatory facilities at our disposal to assure ourselves of that fact. These factors lend themselves all too readily to what is always a temptation: political and social irresponsibility. Now it is easy to decline to join one's fellows in particular issues simply because of the risk of the "smear." The principles at stake in making such a decision are the same as always, but the particular application represents something on which we may have to gain more experience before we can be well guided as to how to act. But one thing is clear: it is a Christian duty to oppose the spread of a philosophy which can impose this ethical question. The vigorous exercise of this

Christian duty is one reason why the most dangerous current exponent of this philosophy has suffered a setback.

Apart from the "public relations" aspect of the problem and its consequent effect on future effectiveness, it is not at all clear as a matter of principle that one may not collaborate even with Communists for the securing of a given object in society. People forget these days that we collaborated with the Soviet Union against Germany and Japan. Collaboration for particular objects has always made strange bedfellows: the real ethical question is what in each collaborator's heart is his motive and the world view from which he operates. And certainly one is ethically free to collaborate with a man whose motives he knows not (as in the case of not knowing that there are any Communists on a particular committee) if he is clear as to the validity of the object and as to his own motives in espousing it. Of course, before actually joining the same association or "board" with persons who have different motives and world views, a man has to take into account the danger that his name and backing may be dishonestly used to further aims and movements with which he is not in accord.

However, these considerations do not end the ethical question for the Christian. We are called upon to be realistic. If in fact people *think* it is wrong to join forces—even unknowingly —with one who turns out to be "Communist-front," that is in itself a factor weighing against such collaboration, in terms of the groups with which one can hope to be effective in the future.

But we should not be overcalculating in this regard. We worship a Lord who said, "Blessed are ye when men speak all manner of evil against you falsely for my sake." We stand in the heritage of people who showed dramatic self-sacrifice in terms of serious issues of the moment: "the goodly fellowship of the prophets, the noble army of martyrs." But the plural phrasing of the *Te Deum* in this regard should remind us that in so doing we would do well to do so in companionship with others so that we are not too readily simply "written off" as "fanatics" or "cranks," thus vitiating the value of the witness. There are times when God calls upon us to sacrifice, but He wants the sacrifice to accomplish something. Jesus Himself chose His occasions of controversy, His occasions of withdrawal.

For the Christian the most obvious corporate possibility of witness is the Church itself. The Church can witness on social and political questions through the corporate action of its representative bodies and through prophetic preaching in the pulpit. But both media involve considerations somewhat different from the factors in the witness and action of the Christian individual. The words of the preacher involve a "speaking for the Church" rather than for "John Jones, Christian." Thus the Church must stand for the principles at stake and not espouse particular solutions or candidates. But this does not mean it should devote itself to the expression of principles without reference to the particular context of the contemporary situation. The preachers and church councils of today, no less than the prophets of old, must condemn *particular* evils within society and must set forth the positive factors involved in right solutions. Only thus can they be a real force for righteousness in the world. In so doing, the Church is not only lending support to ethical fulfillment in particular realms of corporate life; it is also engaging in evangelism. Such action demonstrates that the Church is not "at ease in Zion," that it is not simply one of many institutions in the world in which it lives, but is a standing judgment on the world. Hence the freedom of the pulpit is an important element in the ethical responsibility to the world. This is the opportunity for the Holy Spirit—"Who spake by the prophets"—to express Himself in the world. It is He of whom our Lord said: "When he is come, he will reprove the world of sin, of righteousness, and of judgment." (St. John 16:8.) Thus from an ethical point of view those church polities are best which protect the minister in such freedom of pulpit. When a preacher may say only those things which

E

will be supported by a majority of those listening or by his ecclesiastical superiors, the spirit may be quenched.

But entirely apart from the question of particular legislation and candidates, may not the preacher be wrong, even on the principles at stake? He may. No preacher in any Communion may claim to be infallible, nor may any synod or council. But dedicated spokesmen for the Church, made meet by prayer for guidance as to the meaning of contemporary situations and by familiarity with the Church's tradition in dealing with sin, private and corporate, are not likely to call good "evil" and evil "good." And even though the spokesmen of the Church are from time to time misguided or unwise in their application of moral principle and in their expression of the will of God, nevertheless ferment they initiate as to matters affecting our corporate life in society is itself wholesome. Such ferment may stir men to find better solutions than is represented either by the status quo or by the direction pointed by Church spokesmen; and in any case the ferment stands as witness to the fact that the Christian's citizenship is in heaven and that he is on earth a colonist (to paraphrase St. Paul), seeking constantly to conform this earthly outpost to the standards of what St. Thomas Aquinas has called "our true native land."

CHAPTER XII

Christianity, Democracy, and Communism

What has just been said about the relationship of the Christian in the Church to political and social questions has for the most part presupposed the conditions of a democratic society. This is in part because this book is written by a member of such a society for readers in the same situation; but it is mainly because a democratic society does in fact provide the most fruitful avenue for the fulfillment of the will of God both personally and corporately. However, since this conclusion is altogether too readily assumed by most American Christians it is important to state at this point what we do *not* mean.

We do not mean that there is a simple identification between "the American way of life" and the will of God. Nor do we mean that the particular institutions of democracy in this land or in any other are final and above criticism. And certainly we do not mean that the particular forms of economic organization which have developed in democratic countries necessarily express the perfect will of God as to the weal of all His people here and elsewhere in the world. And in saying that democracy provides the most fruitful opportunity for the fulfillment of the will of God we do not mean to imply for a moment that in every instance, or by and large, this opportunity has been availed of or that there is more holiness and goodness among people in democratic countries and cultures than among those who have lived or who are living under authoritarian regimes. (To conclude this would limit the "calendar of saints" to those living in relatively recent times.)

Nevertheless, it can be said that a society founded upon the principles of democracy does give more *opportunity* to the individual, working alone and in groups, to effectuate the will of God. To appreciate this point fully requires us to recall the very nature and dynamic of Christian ethical action. Human responsibility is grounded in freedom and the greater man's freedom the more he is called upon to exercise individual responsibility. And under God he exercises his responsibility in a sense of vocation: which means to *be* what he is *created* to be—in the image of a triune God; he is to be creative; he is to be redemptive; he is to build community. Obviously he has fuller opportunities to develop his particular talents and gifts (within his particular limitations) in a free society. He is, in such a society, freer to take the means to redeem and heal those around him. And guaranteed freedom of association, speech, press, and religion, he has a greater opportunity to encourage group life inspired by the Spirit, which "bloweth where it listeth." Thus there is greater opportunity in a democracy for new and unexpected forms to arise which will better meet human needs—even forms not embraced within the present delineation of democracy.

Though wrongs there may be—and are—in any democratic society, the opportunity for men, inspired by conscience, to right such wrongs is obviously greater for men who have the ballot and who have freedom to express their opinions and organize groups to implement them. Hence Christians (*as* Christians and not simply as patriotic citizens) have a stake in the maintenance and development of democratic institutions.

But there is another relationship between Christianity and democracy. It is no accident that democracy has historically developed in lands permeated with reformed Christianity and that working democracies are principally found in such lands today. Democracy does not obtain simply because a country has a constitution providing for democratic institutions. There are a number of nations with such constitutions in which, in fact, there is little democracy at all but a more or less powerful dictatorship operating within the shell of a democratic structure. A working democracy comes not from having a constitution, nor from teaching people about that constitution, nor talking about democracy; it comes from having a certain kind of citizen predominant in the life and work of the nation.

What are the characteristic motifs in the lives of individuals which most make them meet to sustain a democracy? This can best be discerned by examining three notions which were deeply ingrained in our American culture at the time our characteristic institutions were formed. (It is true that certain "rationalist" ideas superficially informed some of our forefathers, but these were, in fact, rather late-arrival influences compared with the deep religious convictions in their inheritance.)

1. The first of these convictions was that each man has direct responsibility to God for the management of his life and for the decisions he makes. Social cohesion can be achieved only by a temporal authority from without or a spiritual authority from within. If I recognize in my life the same God my neighbor recognizes in his we can live in peace, order, and co-operativeness without the intervention of a policeman. This is not to say that all those in colonial times were either pious or good, but it is to say that the degree to which external authority was found unnecessary paralleled the degree to which the sense

of individual responsibility to God was a fact working in the citizens. And this is true in any generation.

This sense of individual responsibility for life is, of course, encouraged in a measure by any religious tradition but especially by one in which large place is given to such Reformation doctrines as (1) the sanctity of the common life—under which every man and his calling is under the claim of vocation and every calling is thus potentially a holy one, (2) the relativity of every authority, whether ecclesiastical or civil, and (3) justification by grace through faith, whereby free creative, redemptive, and community-building life is encouraged by the dynamic of thanksgiving for salvation already given (more than by the motive of earning salvation in the life to come).

2. A second important conviction was that God and men last forever—nations come and go. The founders of this nation had no such notion as the finality of the United States; they had just resisted what was then their nation, one to which they were by no means disposed to give final allegiance. Certainly there was here no "America forever" or "my nation right or wrong." They had read their Bibles enough to know that the God of nations alone is final and that He and His covenanted people, rather than nations, abide forever.

> *O where the kings and empires now*
> *Of old, that went and came?*
> *But, Lord, thy Church is praying yet,*
> *A thousand years the same.*

Since they believed in eternal life there was a high evaluation put on the individual. The fact is that every single citizen of the United States will be alive—somewhere—when the whole history of the nation forms a few chapters in some comprehensive history book. This means that each individual, in one sense, is more important than the nation. Hence the Bill of Rights, giving each individual the right to *be* a person, expressing and fulfilling himself as his conscience directs, whether or not a majority finds his views right or convenient.

3. A third relevant conviction of our forefathers was belief in original sin. It is sometimes assumed, looking back through humanist eyes, that the founders thought that men should govern themselves because men are so good. Actually it would be more in accord with the prevailing religious views of the time to say: "We had better govern ourselves because men can be so bad that we dare not have a tyrant." They understood what Lord Acton later so well phrased: "Power corrupts and absolute power corrupts absolutely." They had some actual experience—on the receiving end—of the corruption of power, and their interpretation of the problem was grounded in the Christian understanding of the self-centering tendency of man. Hence the distribution of powers and the system of checks and balances in our government, contrary to the naïve notions of utopian schemes which assume that under the right system men will run things well when given the power to do so.

There are, of course, other influences, both from Christian theology and ethics and from secular sources; but these three are quite basically related to the kind of system we in fact developed, the relationship being both historical and logical. And the fact is that the possibilities of maintaining democratic life today and resisting authoritarian developments without and within depend in large measure on the degree to which these basic motifs can be kept alive in the minds and hearts of those upon whom the maintenance of a free society ultimately rests—namely, the individual citizens. This point is reinforced by a principle asserted in the last chapter, that a nation is in fact no more than the individuals who make it up.

A ready illustration of the relationship between the operation of the democratic process and the actual convictions of the people is found in one aspect of the recent threat to our way of life found in "McCarthyism." Both the Congressional investigatory authority and Congressional immunity are good things. The former gives the elective representatives of the people an opportunity to bring to light and to correct abuses in its own and other branches of the government; the latter allows freedom of expression in the promotion of causes without fear of reprisals. Both can encourage the finest expression of freedom and means whereby tryanny and corruption can be combated. But, in fact, when these two instrumentalities are utilized to air the views and associations of citizens, and where modern media of mass communication bring to every home the charges and assertions of the investigators, there is imperiled the American and Christian principle that a man is presumed to be innocent until proven guilty.

Now it is important to note precisely why this principle is imperiled. It is not that the Congressional investigating committee can do a single thing to a person under investigation. Before he may be punished or denied any of his civil rights there must be an indictment, a trial by a jury of his peers, and a judgment based upon proof beyond a reasonable doubt. So it would appear that nothing has changed. But when in the minds and hearts of a substantial number of our citizens a mere charge by a senator is believed to be establishment of guilt, then actually a good deal is done to someone so placed under suspicion. He cannot get a job; people fear to associate with him; he is in fact "ruined" and "through." This is not the fault of the Constitution and its provisions; this is the fault of the people who—because of their genuine fear of communism or because of their eagerness to "get" people who disagree with them on political and economic issues—have not the spiritual resources to suspend judgment and maintain relationships until in fact there has been an indictment, trial, and establishment of guilt. It is clear that no system works any better than the quality of the attitudes of those who live under the system. This is not to excuse the demagogues who know full well what the public attitude is and use what in themselves are perfectly legitimate processes as a means of denying what really is a fundamental human liberty. But ultimately the blame must fall on the people.

It calls for the finest exercise of Christian ethics in any age to refrain from judgment and maintain fellowship and love with those about whom suspicion has been cast. A temper which seeks to judge, to hate, and to destroy those who hold views other than our own (especially on economic matters which affect one's own interests) is, of course, a very tangible expression of original sin and is nothing new in our own time. But redemption from this very thing will not come by better constitutions or better legislation but by better people. And the maintenance of all the finest elements of our democratic heritage depends on precisely the same thing.

This dependence does not mean that we should *use* religion as a means of supporting our American democracy. This is to fail to put first things first. God and His eternal ends are of importance to the safety of any nation and for the maintenance of its liberties. But much these days which seems friendly to religion, and which is couched in terms of encouraging religion that we may have a better nation, is in fact idolatrous and ultimately blasphemous. The text is, "Seek ye first the kingdom of God and his righteousness and all these other things will be added unto you," not, "Seek ye the kingdom of God and his righteousness *in order that. . . .*" But the fact is that if we do cherish in ourselves, and encourage in our fellow citizens, the right relationship to God and a recognition of His absolute priority we will in fact have a healthier nation. And unhealthy aspects in our national life, whether the increase of juvenile delinquency or the limitation of freedom of individuals, do serve as reminders for us that we must look to the roots wherefrom fresh and healthy fruit can be expected to spring.

These considerations are relevant to what has increasingly been a preoccupation of our people—the defense against communism and communistic ideas. One approach is to burn the books and ruin the suspects within and oppose by military force those without. Another approach is to "buy" the support of the

E*

peoples of the world for our way of life. The former is far from satisfactory because the wheat is pulled up with the tares; the latter has not reaped much reward because the way of life which we would market is all too clearly labeled "Made in U.S.A." In the late and unhappy Korean War it was largely North Koreans and Chinese fighting Americans, not South Koreans fighting Russians. The reason was that the Communists were successful in imbuing the people of another country with a fighting faith, whereas we were not successful in doing so. Non-Russians will fight for communism, but non-Americans will not fight for Americanism. The reason is that communism is a religion, while Americanism is a particular local flowering of a religious faith and of one forgotten by many of the proponents of the -ism. In the long run communism will only be defeated by a better religion, one which can enlist the zeal of its adherents to convert as ably as communism has, one which will express itself in ethical action in a way which is more adequate to man's known needs than communism proves to be.

Communism is, as has often been pointed out, a Judaeo-Christian heresy. It stems from a world view in which something is being worked out in history. For communism, no less than for the Bible, history is seen as having a meaning and an ultimate outcome, and thus it matters what happens in the here and now. In the one it is the victory of God over all pockets of resistance and the willing subjection of all to His reign. In the other it is the rule of the proletariat, having put down all its enemies and thus no longer in need of government or authority. Under either system of thought man's life now has a meaning in so far as it contributes to each of these ends—depending upon which of the two religions is involved. The main difference—and it is an important one—is that a Christian believes that he will personally be a part of the life and fellowship to come, whereas a Communist has no such hope. Thus we have a larger hope and also a greater restraint upon the way we treat people now. Marxists believe that a man dies like a dog; hence they can treat him like one now. If he gets in the way he can be put out of the way. Since as Christians we are committed to the conviction that each man lives forever, his status now is such that we cannot so easily dispose of him with a good conscience. They are logical on their premises; we are logical on ours. The significant difference is in the premises, not in the ensuing logic.

In regard to the ultimate outcome of things, Communists and Christians share one important feature in differentiation from the ordinary American secularist-humanist outlook. The latter feel that if we all work hard enough good things will come. But both the Communists and the Christians believe that "a good time is coming," regardless of the effort or attitude of particular individuals today. When the Communist or the Christian gives his allegiance to his faith he is giving a support to "a sure thing." This "eschatological" confidence gives strength and courage for the here-and-now. It means that one's efforts are ultimately significant and hence meaningful even now. It means that one can approach difficult tasks—judged by others' standards, hopeless tasks—with courage and a sense of victory.

But when we make a contrast between Communist practice and Christian theory we should not assume for a moment that life in the Western democracies fully corresponds to this Christian theory. The fact is that, in regard to the significance of the individual and his opportunities for fulfillment, we often fail also. For example, in the matter of the treatment of the minority racial groups we in fact sometimes lag behind the Iron Curtain countries. Thus in making comparisons of this type it is important for us to recognize that we are comparing Christianity with Marxist theory, not the behavior of Western democracies with the behavior of the Communists. All in all, the behavior of the former may be better than the latter, but by no means do we in the West live up to all the principles which have just been enunciated as the Christian basis for democracy.

And an important safeguard against our indulging in comparisons to the enhancement of our own pride is the recognition that communism would not exist in so many places in the world had we in Western society sufficiently taken care of the pressing needs of the underprivileged. In this sense communism is a judgment upon us even as the Assyrians were "the rod of God."

But communism is a judgment upon us in even a more serious way. The reason we find communism so terrifying corresponds to the fear a child has of his magnified shadow thrown on the wall. Actually we too have a culture largely centered upon material things. We do not philosophize about it in terms of a materialistic dialectic; we simply live things out that way. What matters most in the hearts of many of our people is the making of money and the production of things. We are terrified when we see a thoroughgoing system dedicated to what actually is consciously or unconsciously the predominant motif for most of our people. The fact is that communism is our own materialism "writ large": communism is secularism taken seriously.

There are those who take comfort in the fact that when all is said and done we are superior to the Communists because they are "godless," whereas we believe in God. We need to take a more careful look at our own situation. We are not made a people of God simply because we talk about God, simply because we engrave "In God we trust" on our coins, or because we now have added "under God" to the pledge of allegiance to the flag, or even because a lot of us attend church. Here we are taken back to the considerations in Chapter II. A man's god is whatever is first in his life. Who is the more godless, a man who openly affirms he is not a believer in God or the man who openly affirms with his lips that he believes in God but lives his life out in the adoration of the god of self, the god of money, the god of prestige, or the god of production?

Thus what we need to oppose communism successfully is not only a recognition of the basic superiority of our own loyalties in the knowledge that they are grounded in the right attitudes toward God. We need *actually* to place God at the center of things. Thus we will be empowered as a people to sustain the terrible and wonderful burden of a democracy, in co-operation with our neighbors, through the internal disciplines sustained by our final allegiance to God. This will keep alive our respect for individuality and our concern for the total fulfillment of all men because they, like ourselves, are made in the image of God and have an eternal destiny. Meanwhile we will be soberly concerned as to the distribution of power in government because we are aware of the proneness of man to sin, especially when girded with power.

The moment we have said this—namely, that by a return to the foundation principles upon which our democracy rests we will strengthen this system as against the threat of communism without and within—we seem to be suggesting that we should "use" Christianity to bolster our particular way of life. As has already been indicated, this is really to put something ahead of God—namely, "our way of life"—and to regard God as a means in relation thereto. Again a very fine line has to be drawn, but it is an important line. If that which we regard as of highest value is best sustained by Christian allegiance, then this should properly serve as a reminder to us of the seriousness of our departure as a people from these basic Christian foundations. But, in returning to them, true religion requires that we worship and serve God *for His own sake,* and then in fact all these other things "will be added" unto us.

The increasing "official piety" of politicians and of patriotic organizations oversimplifies the whole matter in urging that we "return" to God. This overlooks the fact that the true God is not primarily concerned with being an endorser of our way of life; all sons of men are His children, and indeed He stands in judgment upon even the best of our way of life, let alone the worst. The thought of "going back" to God is often more of a folk nostalgia than a serious personal commitment, in head and heart, to a God who judges as well as saves. It is often "the American way of life" that is being deified—with God as an acolyte in its worship.

CHAPTER XIII

Sex, Marriage, and the Family

In the relationship between absolute and contingent loyalties the family is a microcosm of the State. The same Lord who said, "A man shall leave father and mother and cleave to his wife," asserted the priority of God over the claims of father and mother and of wife and children: "Who are my mother and brothers? Those who hear the word of God and keep it." The paradox can be resolved only in terms of priorities of allegiance: God comes first; allegiance to family normally comes second. But the first priority may sometimes require us to put other things ahead of family—such as military service to one's nation and the taking of time away from our families to further certain causes for the Kingdom of God.

Christ, endorsing the approach of the Book of Genesis, grounds the family relationship in the natural order: "Have ye not read, that He which made them at the beginning made them male and female, and said, For this cause shall a man leave father and mother and shall cleave to his wife: and they twain shall be one flesh? Wherefore they are no more twain, but one flesh." To this extent marriage and the creation of a family are trans-ethical. Only under very unusual circumstances should a man marry a woman only because he feels he *ought* to. He should marry her because he is in love with her; and no one— not even God—can successfully command that one person have romantic love for another. So two aspects of the marriage relation cannot be encompassed by any system of ethics: the natural fact of sex differentiation and its implications, and the feeling of romantic love—the appearance and disappearance of which follows no rational laws.

The fact that ethics is not primarily involved in these factors has caused many people—quite ethical in intent—to assume that there is no "ought" level involved in the matter. They assume that a person will marry the person with whom he is in love and that, conversely, if he falls out of love with her into love with someone else, he will divorce the one and marry the other. Many carry this simple principle further and, while regarding sexual promiscuity or sex for its own sake as unethical, endorse sexual relations outside of marriage if the participants "love" each other, "sincerity" being the only test. In part this attitude of a segment of modern life is a reaction from an opposite view which is still widely prevalent, an attitude which ties up sex altogether too much with ethics, regarding, for example, the sexual relationship as essentially ignoble even in the marriage relation (or at least less noble than abstinence therefrom) and any ecstatic interest in the visible relationship as shameful, even going so far as to categorize intercourse as a "wifely duty." Concurrent with this attitude, though sometimes separate from it, has been a view of marriage which has emphasized social and practical factors in the choice, with considerable distrust of romantic love.

We will be helped in our critique of these two diverse attitudes and in our understanding of the place Christian ethics in fact has in the sex and marriage relationship if we distinguish three kinds of love—all of which in English are confusingly embraced within the single word "love."

In the Greek there are three words for love: *eros, philia,* and *agapé. Eros* is the hardest to encompass within a definition, because it, of the three, is the least rational in nature. *Eros* is the love of the other because of the other's lovableness (real or apparent). It seeks to possess the other, to have and to hold. While its richest and most ecstatic fulfillment is in the sexual relationship, it is actually much broader, both in its scope and its means of expression. It is not, in fact, limited to persons of the opposite sex or to persons as to whom there might be any thought of sexual relationship. We have a degree of *eros* love for many people —parents, friends, and even casual acquaintances—as we respond in respect, enthusiasm, and interest to various aspects of their make-up and personality; we express this love erotically (in a measure at least) in the natural warmth of a handshake or a slap on the back or in the mere desire to be with the other person. Many rational factors affect our responsive decision as to whom we wish to be with, but essentially the response itself is trans-ethical; as we have seen, it cannot be commanded. We like people or we don't, and we like some people much better than we like others.

Normally, of course, *eros* love has its most intense emotional implications in the case of the love of persons of the opposite sex. The intensity and persistence of this affection may be strong enough that there is a desire to spend one's whole life with the object of the love. Many of the external symbols of the various levels of *eros*—especially those on the less intense levels—are in fact arbitrary, varying in different cultures. Though all utilize some form of physical contact, some peoples brush cheeks, others touch hands, others rub noses. However, in the case of the more intense romantic attachment between persons of the opposite sex the bodily fulfillment in all times and cultures has been sexual intercourse and its attendant love play.

Eros and its attendant desires, though wonderful—in the strict sense of that word, are evanescent when not undergirded by a lifelong commitment which enables the couple to enter deeply into each other's personalities and directions. Even in marriage —and in the best of marriages—there are parentheses in attraction to, and desire for, the other. Some of the causes for this are obvious: a hurt dealt by one or the other, distraction, or preoccupation with other things or persons. Other causes are not quite so evident, resting on unconscious factors, perhaps psychosomatic ones. *Eros* alone is not a dependable basis for marriage or any other sustaining relationship—though, except in unusual circumstances, no marriage should be undertaken without it and no one in a marriage should be content with a situation in which it is not present.

Philia is love for the other because of some third person, object, cause, or interest to which the two are mutually devoted. It too has a broader scope than two persons of opposite sex. It can exist between any two people who are mutually attracted by the same things. It may be that the two are fond of tennis, are wrapped up in some movement, or even share the same hatreds (though the latter is an undesirable, and in the long run destructive, basis for liaison). While this kind of love does have a broad scope, it exists most strongly where there is a basis of permanent tie, and it is especially evident in marriage where almost every event or important interest in the life of one is or can be a concern of the other. But it too is unreliable as a basis of lifelong marriage. Interest can fade; ennui can destroy former enthusiasms; causes can fail or lose their significance; persons to whom the two are devoted can become alienated or die. Even the most fruitful source of *philia* love between spouses, namely, common devotion to their children, can fail: children can die or tragically disappoint their parents, and they are capable of displaying embittering ingratitude.

Agapé is difficult to define, but it can readily enough be described. It can operate all along in a situation, but its character may not be evident when *eros* or *philia* are also in the picture, because they supply sufficient explanation for the love bestowed. But the operation of *agapé* is evident when the other does not appear to be lovable and when mutual interests do not seem to inspire. *Agapé* is a love of the other not because of the other's lovableness, or because of some outside source, but because of the other's *need* of love. It is a concern for the other's best interest when no benefit accrues to the lover and no response is counted on.

A husband has grown wayward. At first this may heighten the *eros* love of his wife for him, since her possession of him is threatened (for there is a strange interlocking of the negative trait of jealousy and the positive factor of *eros*). But the continuance of disappointment and frustration—and perhaps of loneliness—may well mean the destruction of *eros*. This of course becomes evident enough to him; and yet his position at this point is in one way more difficult than hers. Should he— either out of a sense of duty or a revival of his own *eros* love for his wife—wish to return to the relationship, he may nevertheless be fearful that his overtures will be rebuffed, that he will not be accepted, or that his acceptance will be intermixed with misgivings and loss of trust in the future and accompanied by a patronizing spirit and manner. Thus he is the more likely to take comfort in the companion who has distracted him in the first place. There he feels surer of himself. The two are tied together at least by their sense of guilt, whereas he would not have this —and perhaps at this point nothing else—as a common basis of feeling with his wife. Should she be able to look beyond her own hatred and resentment and sense his real need of the moment and take the risk of meeting him on his own level and showing love for him, taking the hurt of the situation into herself and thus, from her side, taking up the slack between them, this would be *agapé* love. Of course, in so doing, she takes the risk of rebuff, but this fear is part of the hurt she is willing to take. And often enough in such a situation his need is met, the situation is healed, and *eros* love is revived—indeed intensified because of this deep experience.

Or: A wife is going through change of life and she shows signs of tenseness and irritability—and underneath there is a growing sense of insecurity. Simply on an *eros* basis it is likely her husband will find her less attractive, less lovable. If he is therefore less attracted and less loving her anxiety will mount and her tenseness and "snappiness" increase. Thus, in turn, he is all the less attracted, all the less loving. This vicious circle may even lead into interest in someone else or a greater preoccupation with his work or other interests. But if perchance he senses the situation and seeks to meet her need of support and affection with even greater attention, it may well be that the whole thing will amount to nothing at all, since menopause is to such a considerable degree psychosomatic in its nature. In any case, her response to his love may well bring a new depth into the marriage relationship.

This kind of love looks, on the face of it, much like a particular form of calculatedness which is almost its exact opposite and which generally will have much less satisfactory results. If one spouse puts on a front of interest *in order that* the other may react in certain ways there is a superior and contrived quality about the love bestowed which all too easily reveals itself and undermines the chance of a fruitful outcome. In any case, whatever its prudential value in some circumstances, this is not *agapé* love.

This points to what the nature and source of this love really is. All things have a cause, including love. What is the true cause of *agapé* love? It is not what the philosophers call a "final" cause, i.e., it is not something done because of the anticipated result. Nor is there any apparent "effective" cause; there is present neither the lovableness of the object nor the interest in some third person or thing.

We are closer to discerning the true cause of *agapé* when we recognize that this love found its way into Western civilization only through the Judaeo-Christian tradition. The Greek language had no word for it: the word *agapé* was actually an archaic synonym for *eros* which St. Paul and the author (or authors) of the

Fourth Gospel and the Johannine epistles "dusted off" (as it were) and used for this new kind of love. In fact, the famous passage in I Corinthians 13 is an elaborate definition of it for a culture that knew nothing of it heretofore. It is this love (translated somewhat quaintly as "charity" in the King James version) that "suffereth long, and is kind . . . envieth not . . . vaunteth not itself, is not puffed up, does not behave itself unseemly, seeketh not her own, is not easily provoked, thinketh no evil; rejoiceth not in iniquity, but rejoiceth in the truth; beareth all things, believeth all things, hopeth all things, and endureth all things." It is this love that "never faileth."

We get a strong hint of its import in the Old Testament book of Hosea. There the prophet's wife Gomer has been promiscuous and after their separation falls on such evil days that she is to be sold as a slave on the auction block. Her husband buys her back, takes her to himself, taking the hurt of both the social and personal situation when redeeming her and the marriage. Then the prophet uses this painful period of his life, which was well known to the community, as a basis of pointing to the *Source* of such love: he says in effect, "God is like that toward us." But it is in the New Testament—especially in the central mighty act which it records, the saving passion and death of Jesus Christ—that we see demonstrated most vividly what the source of *agapé* is. Not only in this supreme moment but through His entire life we see God, who in Christ translated Himself into the language of a human life, showing forth *agapé* love toward us: "God *so* loved the world. . . ."

As we have seen, God here takes up the hurt of our situation, takes up the slack between Himself and us, loves us though unlovable, accepts us though unacceptable. Thus the source of *agapé* love is gratitude for the fact that we have already been loved this way. This is why it needs no reward; this is why it does not depend upon the response from the one so loved; this is how it can be based upon the other's need of love and not upon the other's lovableness.

Obviously *agapé* is not without result in the life and responses of the one loved when so accepted. The one so loved has now a footing on which to stand and can more readily become that which he is accepted as being. He, in turn, may gratefully respond to this kind of love—without fear of rebuff or rejection. The unlovely when loved can become lovable.

Agapé is not supposed to take the place of *eros* and *philia* in a marriage. In fact, time and time again it fortifies these other types of love. In the case of the latter one may, through *agapé*, consciously develop an expressed concern with an interest that the spouse has, and almost inevitably as a result a genuine interest in it will arise. A wife may care nothing for baseball, which is the dominant hobby of her husband; but if she tries to understand what is going on at the game and expresses enthusiasm at the right points she will find that she can, in a measure, actually share the interest her husband has. And *eros* generally returns to a situation whence it has fled when *agapé* love has filled the gap which for some reason or other has appeared. More particularly in the sexual relationship itself a husband may restrain his full emotional involvement in the act out of *agapé* concern for his wife's fulfillment, which may be—and generally is—more difficult; but her appreciative responses will actually heighten the whole *eros* relationship. *Agapé* is related to *eros* and *philia* like the crank on old-fashioned cars. When the battery was run down the motor could be started by cranking the car; but once the motor was running the battery would build up and the crank could be dispensed with until the next crisis; and meanwhile it was always there. The figure used may give the impression that *agapé* is something for occasional use (and here the crank analogy breaks down); actually *agapé* in a marriage, as a constant response to the love of God, can afford (sometimes consciously, sometimes unconsciously) a support for the integration of every relationship and for every expression of the other kinds of love.

Because this love is so important in a marriage it is not surprising—in this centrifugal age in which we live—that marriages in which the spouses are in active touch with the Source of *agapé* love are, statistically speaking, more likely to be successful. Studies have shown that marriages in which the couples have an active religious faith are two to two and a half times more successful than those which do not (judging by the figures on separation or divorce). But entirely apart from this pragmatic test, it is obvious that a marriage which has this element—constantly reinforced by contact with the Source of the reinforcement—is bound to be richer and fuller than one which may from time to time reflect the exercise of this love (because of the general cultural milieu in which it still forms an important part because of the Christian heritage of our civilization) but without the constant "refueling" which active Christan allegiance affords.

The emphasis of Christianity on *agapé* love, and the fact that it is the uniquely *Christian* love,·is by no means a devaluation of *eros* love. Though this conclusion is logically obvious enough, it needs saying because significant parts of the Christian Church at one time or another have in fact "played down" *eros* and have exalted other ideals at its expense.

In the Middle Ages arose the notion that the sexual relationship, being carnal, was less worthy than abstinence from this relationship under vows of celibacy, such abstinence being viewed as pleasing to God and making for extra merit before Him. The exaltation of virginity still has a large place in Roman Catholic thought, as is evidenced by the recent papal encyclical on the subject. To this day a voluntary vow, even within marriage, to abstain from intercourse is regarded in that tradition as a meritorious act.

American Protestant Christianity also has shown signs of a negative view toward sex, having been influenced in this direction both by Puritan and by later pietistic influences. This negativism has had a widespread impact upon the unconscious as well as the conscious thought of Americans inside and outside of the

Church, with the result that in American culture the word "sin" almost inevitably evokes in the mind a picture of sex and other fleshly joys.

So successful have been the proponents of such views over the years that they have unconsciously affected many people who do not hold to the traditions out of which they have sprung, with the result that there is widespread difficulty in sexual adjustment in marriage. Often people who are sufficiently emancipated intellectually along these lines find it difficult to give themselves unreservedly and ecstatically to something that 'way down underneath—due to social conditioning—they feel to be unclean and unworthy. On the other hand, the hidden sense of guilt about sex has often driven to excess those who have really decided to cut loose from the taboos. The feeling that, since one is a sinner anyway, one might as well sin consistently, and with relish, expresses an inner feeling not often consciously analyzed. And, because many people in our land have interpreted religion principally in terms of "anti-joy," many naturally expressive people have rejected it out of hand and thus lost the basis for the right direction in the use of the joys of life and the basis for proper limitation in their exercise. Thus a right view toward this whole matter is important both for better fulfillment and for better discipline.

Whence the negativism regarding sex? It all traces back to a false relationship between the contrasts of spirit/flesh and good/bad. It is necessary (perhaps only semantically) to distinguish between flesh and spirit and actually necessary to distinguish good and bad. But it is a serious heresy to associate spirit with good and flesh with bad.* The oriental religions usually do make

---

*Adding to the confusion is the fact that the King James version translates the word *sarx* as *flesh*. Actually *sarx* means the downward tendencies of spirit—which can use flesh for their fulfillment. Thus *sarx* has a quite different meaning from *soma*, usually translated *body*, with neutral ethical implications. See the author's *Beyond Anxiety* (Scribner's, 1954), pp. 47–49.

this distinction—and thoroughgoingly: the more spirit and the less flesh figuring in a man's life the better. A man's final hope is that he will become so spiritual that he will escape entirely from fleshly life and be absorbed into the oversoul. But biblical religion, when it is true to its heritage, does not so view the relationship of the spirit and the flesh, nor does it view man's destiny in terms of his becoming all spirit. Hence in the Christian tradition the credal affirmation is not "the immortality of the soul" but "the resurrection of the body." This, of course, does not refer to the present body (which changes every seven years) but rather asserts that in the life to come man's spirit will be *embodied*, that is, given appropriate means of expression, communication, and fulfillment, leaving him an individual—not less himself but more himself than ever. Thus it is not that the spirit is good and the flesh bad; in fact, it is nearer the reverse: it is the spirit that can be bad, and the flesh can be utilized to carry out either good or bad intentions and directions. But the flesh itself is not merely neutral in value: it is *good* because it is the gift of God, and its joys are good because God rejoices in our joy, which He has made possible for us. Thus spirit is not better than flesh: *the true good is spirit and flesh functioning together in a right direction, utilized in a sense of vocation.*

Actually in the good life the two are sacramentally united, the flesh being a means of grace, an outward and visible sign of inward and spiritual reality. The flesh can both express the spirit and be a means for furthering and developing the spirit. While obviously we are called to be more spiritual we are not called thereby to be less fleshly; there is no correlation between these two directions.

Sexual intercourse is meant to be a sacrament. A sacrament, of course, is "an outward and visible sign of an inward and spiritual grace." The inward and spiritual requisite is the total and permanent pooling of hopes and fears, of strengths and weaknesses. The outward and visible sign is, as in other sacraments, both expression of spirit and means of grace. The sexual relationship expresses the love and commitment the couple already possesses; it also strengthens and inspires that commitment.

Thus marriage is not in a second place ethically to virginity, nor is a marriage better which is less "physical." The choice between married life and celibacy and the choice of occasions of sexual expression within marriage are not to be determined by the question of how spiritual or physical the relationship is but rather by a sense of vocation. If a man would be a celibate, it should be because he feels that he can best serve God in this way, not because thereby he can avoid physical relationships and thus "please God." And if restraints are exercised within marriage, it should be precisely on the same basis. A preoccupation with sex within marriage would be wrong, not because any individual act or particular form the relationship takes is in itself more unworthy, but rather because a spouse is not keeping the whole relationship and one's other relationships in due proportion.

Because the sexual relationship is a sacrament there is open the possibility of sacrilege. In our culture we have generally taught young people that sexual intercourse is wrong and the use of it within marriage is to be regarded as a sort of exception, like a special license to park one's car illegally. Actually we should not have been saying that sex is a bad thing; we should have been stressing that sex is a good thing, that it is a sacrament and therefore should not be used sacrilegiously. When the outward and visible sign is entered into without the inward and spiritual commitment, then this, as in the case of other sacraments, is the very meaning of sacrilege. Sex apart from marriage is wrong, not because sex is bad, but because it is so good. There are other reasons for abstinence, such as danger of social involvements, of disease, or of childbirth, but the only *ethical* basis that can be proclaimed, without expense to the status of this relationship *within* marriage, is that indulging in relations without the total commitment which marriage represents is to use a good thing in a wrong way, and the gravity of the wrong is in direct proportion to the degree of the goodness of this relationship. Since it is very good its misuse is very bad.

To return to marriage, obviously one of the purposes of this relationship is procreation. Some have regarded this as the only real purpose, though with the concession that the couple's joy in each other may not be unintended by the Creator. This misconception, which overlooks or downgrades the sacramental function, leads to confusion as to the propriety of the limitation of the procreative activity. Those who hold the use of contraceptive devices to be sinful in any and all circumstances argue that, since *the* purpose of the act is procreation, to thwart that purpose is unnatural. Granted the premise, the conclusion is sound enough. But if the relationship has two purposes, one a procreative and one a sacramental function, then when the first purpose is inappropriate, under a sense of vocation, the attempt to limit the results to the second function still leaves us with an important natural function being fulfilled. The use of scientific means to alter, limit, and direct bodily functions is accepted by everyone in other realms: the existence of barbers' shears and nail files remind us of this as much as the surgeon's scalpel or the physician's prescription blank. In fact, a part of man's obligation to live under vocation is to use his mind to seek, so far as possible, to achieve by the means at his disposal those ends which he believes represent the will of God for his life.

There is no law from on high which can tell a given couple how many children they ought to have. That decision they must make in the light of their whole situation, with purity of heart and with practicality of mind. Once having made the decision, they are obligated, in this realm as well as in any other, to use the best means possible to achieve it. Should the decision be to limit—for the time being or for good—the procreative function, these same factors will not usually afford a basis for limiting the sacramental function in a marriage. Therefore, it would be wrong to use abstinence as the means of birth control, effective as it is as a limitation on procreation, when other means are available which save the sacramental function while putting in abeyance the procreative one.

As to when a couple should or should not have a child, we are thrown back to the basic considerations of vocation. Certainly the building of a family should normally be a positive aim; but even here the bringing of a new life into being should be the conscious and free act of those vocated under God and not simply something that happens by mere chance or because thought has not been taken as to the matter. And where the minimum economic, psychological, and physical conditions are not available, or anticipatable in the near future, it would be wrong not to take such steps as will make childbirth unlikely. A responsible ethic of freedom in vocation can come out with no other conclusion.

It is too late in this book to take too seriously the objection that men will abuse this freedom or will selfishly decide to limit childbirth. This most certainly some will do; but the answer is not a legalistic ethic but greater soul-searching toward the end of purity of heart. The only answer finally is a sense of vocation about responsibility as married persons and as actual or potential parents. If this sense of vocation does not exist the couple will not make the best parents in any case. If it does exist we can trust them to make their decision about childbirth as decisions under God.

Viewing the sexual relationship as a sacrament, we defined the "inward and spiritual" part as total commitment of lives "for better, for worse, for richer, for poorer, in sickness and in health." But many people sincerely ask, "Are there not situations short of marriage in which there is a sufficient measure of devotion and sincerity that sexual intercourse is appropriate —and a good and beautiful thing rather than a sinful thing?"

In answering this question we have to recognize the vast difference between a casual relation—e.g., with a prostitute—and relationships entered into between persons who have real love for each other but who, for one reason or another, are not in a position to marry. But, paradoxically enough, while the former relationship is more sacrilegious than the latter (which actually partakes of the nature of a sacrament), the latter threatens more damage to the personalities involved than the former. The higher the degree of actual involvement short of marriage, the greater the potential harm to those engaged in intercourse with each other. The fact is that in a casual or a purchased relationship there may be little permanent effect upon the inner side of the participants, whereas when the relationship is the expression of a general and abiding devotion it cannot help but in turn fan the flames of that devotion, on the one hand, and create hidden—if not overt—forms of anxiety, on the other.

Actually, short of marriage there is not total commitment. And the lack of commitment makes the increasing closeness an increasing ground of anxiety. This anxiety often expresses itself in ways not related to the actual activity of intercourse, and often tensions increase, jealousies are heightened, the uncertainty of the future is magnified, and frustrations develop (due to what is generally an inability to enjoy the relationship in a sense of security), with the result that separation, rather than marriage, is often the result. If the rupture does occur, the participants are never quite the same again. An aching void is found in their hearts, one often filled with bitterness and cynicism. Since in all our ethical choices we are responsible for what we make of ourselves in the continuing service of God and our fellows, we are called to avoid those things which may distort our personalities, those things which invite frustrations. So, while we do not classify together harlotry and the relationships of loved ones, each for its own reasons is a sin, the former because it is boldly sacrilegious in the use of an outward and visible sign which has no relationship to the meaning for which it was ordained, and the latter because it expresses somewhat less than the appropriate inward and spiritual side—namely, total commitment—and hence frustration and grief are too easily invited.

Fear of childbirth is a less powerful deterrent these days than heretofore, but actually there is a great difference between the attitude of a married couple practicing birth control because of a decision of conscience and an unmarried couple practicing it. The married couple accepts the responsibilities of the relationship and knows that childbirth is a logical and beautiful fruitage of the relationship. Thus, even during a period when it has seemed the best wisdom not to increase the family, the responsibility for any fruitage is presupposed. In other words, the fact is that if—in spite of all plans for the contrary—a child is born, the child will come into a permanent and abiding context. But in the case of the unmarried couple there is all along the recognition that if a child is born there is no place for it. Involved in this unconscious and suppressed fear is more than the fear of inconvenience; there is the sense that the relationship lacks the commitment which is in fact appropriate to it, a commitment ready and able to receive and welcome whatever happens to be the outcome. This, more than anything else, reveals the wrong of sexual relationships apart from marriage.

We have talked of a "total and permanent pooling." What, then, of divorce? Is it ever right to terminate a marriage? And if it is terminated, are the partners free to remarry? Here the civil law varies from area to area, and the canon law of the Church has varied in each tradition in different times—all because we are dealing with one of the most difficult paradoxes of Christian ethics. Having mentioned the civil law simply as a reflection of the complication of the problem, we will make no further mention of it because, according to our analysis, it is not ultimately the test for the Christian.

Obviously the will of God for marriage is that it should be for life. We have the Lord's word for that. Thus, when marriage fails, there is always sin on the part of one party or both—usually of both. Less than the will of God has been fulfilled. A short-term liaison or "companionate marriage" falls short of providing that total commitment which is the inner condition of the outward relationship. The damage to each personality through a separation when there has been a close grafting of lives, and the insecurity which undermines the lives of children, is so grave that nothing less than marriage for the whole life long represents the will of God. And those who have been blessed with such a marriage to the end of their days experience a mature union on this earth that partakes of the joys of Heaven.

But sin is a fact in the world, and when the conditions for such continued union have failed, when one or both parties have given themselves to others, or displayed continued cruelty and failure of sympathy, the time may come when the question is not "What is the ideal?" but "What is the lesser of two evils?" And divorce may sometimes be the lesser of two evils: the continuance of the marriage may cause greater damage to the personalities involved and greater insecurity for the children than its termination. Thus if a spouse, repentant for his share in the wrong situation, yet concludes sincerely that under the circumstances a divorce is *the less wrong action,* then in the situation it is *the right action.* True, if both parties are under religious influences, and are really seeking to do the will of God, they can with patience and grace work out almost any situation and should seek to do so before considering separation. But often one of the parties has never known or has abandoned the restraints which can dispose his mind and heart to grace, and if the situation is hopeless enough long enough the other party has no choice but to seek to build a new life, one to be lived apart from the erstwhile spouse.

Obviously separation or divorce is not proper simply because one spouse has found someone whom he deems more attractive. Interest in and even passion for another person may well enter the picture, just from a natural responsiveness: a man is not blinded or made unresponsive to anyone but his wife simply because of the marriage ceremony. But preoccupation with such natural affections is in itself sinful because it leads to the furtherance of passions which may well deflect the will and destroy existing commitments. A decision to marry is a decision to go *this* way and not *that:* it is a deliberate restriction of the possibilities of one's emotional fulfillment. Under no system of ethics is it conceivable that a man is justified in leaving his wife to marry another.

However, after a divorce which has seemed to represent on its own footing the lesser of two evils, may one then be open to love for another, a love which may be fulfilled in marriage? Here an important distinction must be made. There are instances in which the first "marriage" was not in fact a marriage at all: thus both the State and the Church recognize the category of *annulment*. The grounds of annulment vary in various legal and ecclesiastical traditions, but the theory of it has been rather constant. If the conditions necessary for marriage have been lacking *ab initio,* then the marriage does not exist, and such may be declared by civil and/or ecclesiastical authority. A marriage entered into because of fraud or duress, a union of persons not eligible to marry because of age, or inadequate mental or physical condition, or "mistaken identity" (a rare circumstance, it would seem), is by no tradition regarded as an impediment to a new union. In such case, the "second" marriage is in fact the first. However, when such conditions precedent do not exist, where there really was a first marriage, but one which has failed and was terminated by divorce, a more complicated question is presented when the ethics of remarriage is considered.

In terms of the ideal of the will of God, one can say at the outset that such second marriages ought not to be. But neither ought the divorce to have occurred, which means in turn that the first marriage should not have failed. So even to ask the question about remarriage is to presuppose a sinful situation, one as to which the person asking the question (for himself) ought to feel a sense of repentance and a sense of guilt. However, a sense of guilt and repentance is answered by justification: by God's new acceptance of us, though unacceptable. And hence a new ethical question now arises: *granted* the failure of the first marriage and the responsibility of both spouses for it, what is now the will of God for the divorced persons?

To take a hard case: Let us assume that a young lady of eighteen, because of weak moral standards, fell in love with a man of low character, who very soon began to demonstrate the same by his promiscuity abroad and his cruelty at home. Suppose a wrestling of conscience led her to seek a divorce and procure it. Her former spouse marries one of his mistresses. She is now twenty-one, is much chastened by the experience, and her standards are elevated thereby. She now meets a fine person to whom she seems ideally suited, and they both wish to live their lives out together under God. The ethical question is not "Should the first marriage have occurred?" or "Should it have failed?" or "Should she have procured a divorce?" That is all over. This is the only relevant question now: is it the will of God that she go through the rest of her life single or as married and as the mother of children? Again, we are not asking the ideal question; we are asking, "What is the lesser of two evils?"—since already evil has entered the picture, though in this case the evil has been repented of. The perfect will of God may not be fulfilled in the situation; it is too late for that: The question is, "What is the nearest thing to the will of God, the greatest good now possible?" It seems clear enough in such a case (although by no means in all cases) that she should marry and receive the blessing of God on the union.

This analysis is not in contradiction to the clear word of Jesus about the permanence of marriage and about the wrong of remarriage. His word does indeed state the right and ideal situation, but since the ideal situation has not happened, and clearly now cannot happen, the question is, "What is the will of God now?" Jesus said, "What God hath joined together let no man put asunder." But what if man has put it asunder? Then what?

There would obviously seem to be situations in which the will of God would be better furthered by marriage than by decades of single life on the part of those not really called to celibacy as a special way of life. A particular religious tradition may feel that its dual task of witnessing to the ideal—the permanence of marriage—and of pastorally meeting the needs of individuals in their actual situations requires the inconsistency of refusing to provide a church wedding and at the same time readmitting the couple to communion with the Church after they have in fact remarried—when they have demonstrated their desire to have a Christian union. But as to the actual *ethics* of the decision that the couple has to make, it would seem that there may be no flat rule against remarriage consistent with the Christian ethic which in all other realms of life bids us choose the better of two less than ideal situations, humbly recognizing the part that our own fault may have played in creating a situation where such a choice becomes relevant.

It is argued by some that a young lady like the one in the illustration should spend the rest of her life single in order to witness to the principle of the permanence of marriage. However, there are other elements of the Christian religion to which we must also witness; namely, the forgiveness of God and the new joy and fulfillment He can bring into our lives after forgiveness. A successful marriage for life is a witness to God's will. But a successful Christian marriage after the failure of the first is also a witness to the power of God who makes all things new.

But obviously the situation is more ideal when this latter problem need not be raised. And that the ideal may more and more be achieved in marriage—one marriage, and for life—nothing could be more important than the development of the highest standards of choice and the grounding of the marriage

F

from the beginning in the Christian faith so that its resources, especially of *agapé* love and the inspiration of the Holy Spirit in the Christian community, may sustain the marriage from the beginning and constantly heal such wounds as may be suffered as the marriage progresses. The difficulty with many marriages is not that people do not get what they want in a mate, but that they *do* get what they want—having wanted the wrong things. And a second basis of tragedy is that, having a spouse with whom a fine marriage could have worked out, they fail to nourish the marriage with the resources which God provides in Christ through the love which comes from Him and is meant to be re-expressed in our earthly relationships. That is why any failure in a marriage is sin and why any questions of re-marriage are questions asked in a sinful situation. Hence one of the surest bases for a successful second marriage is a genuine recognition of the initial inadequacy of standards of choice and the subsequent failure of Christian love, which has caused the possibility of a second marriage to arise.

CHAPTER XIV

Christian Love in One-to-One Relationships

At length we take up what for many people is regarded as virtually the whole of ethics: the way one person treats another. This is the realm people are thinking of when they affirm that they simply live by the Golden Rule. They may be doing so or they may not, but at least here there is the possibility of simple and direct application of "the ethics of Jesus," by which men mean the maxims of the Sermon on the Mount. Here it would seem that the law of love may have an unambiguous exercise. Examples such as the Bishop's candlesticks and Jean Valjean, and St. Martin dividing his coat with a beggar, spring to mind.

But first we must recognize that the periphery of this area is narrower than most people suppose. Life is so interlocked that few opportunities for action or restraint involve only two people. If a man demands my coat and I accede and give my cloak also I may be forced, in order to continue to get back and forth to my work, to purchase these items with money which is needed for clothing for my children. The moment the claims of others enter the picture, directly or indirectly, the apparent simplicity of Christ's law becomes complex.

Does this mean that the teaching of Christ is irrelevant except in strictly "one-to-one" relationships? We have already answered that in the negative. Even in more complex situations the absolutes serve as the measuring rod by which we discern what the relevant claims are in a situation and the relative ethical quality of alternative solutions under consideration.

But there is an area in which the absolute demands can express themselves in simplicity matching their words; and this is not only an important realm of ethical action for its own sake but also serves as the constant reminder of the interests at stake in the more complex situations. The interconnection between interpersonal conduct and attitude and action on the broader social issues is made evident to us by our natural antipathy to the views of people who personally are unkind. And our intuitive response in this regard is at least in part sound: if the proponent of a cause is insensitive to personal feelings and needs it is likely that the evaluation of factors which led him to his convictions has been unbalanced.

For present purposes we should theoretically isolate the strictly one-to-one relationship. But practically we cannot so narrow the periphery. In every relationship—save that between two persons on a desert island for life—there are collateral factors. There are virtually always other relationships and responsibilities in the picture. Yet there are occasions in which the one-to-one relationship *predominates* sufficiently for us to perceive the operation of the absolute demands.

The call of vocation and the law of love is here focused in terms of the second great commandment: "Thou shalt love thy neighbor as thyself." Already we have analyzed the ambiguous word love. Here the love is *agapé*, not *eros* or *philia*. A man may not by command love another in any other sense. This is a command to love people we may not like, whose company we may not enjoy. The scope of *agapé* in the commandment is pointed up by the cognate command, "Do unto others as you would have them do unto you." *Agapé* is a concern for the true interests of the other issuing in action. Either way the injunction is phrased there is a reference to the self as norm. This, at the least, is meant to insure that one takes interests of the other as seriously as he takes his own interests and that he seeks for the other at least what he seeks for himself. And this is considerably ahead of the performance of most of us. But more is implied. Under judgment is one's own priority scale of values. If intoxication is a prime value for a man, the maintenance of an amply supplied bar for his alcoholic acquaintances may leave something to be desired in ethical fulfillment, though it is literally doing for others as he would have them do for him. So the observance of the second commandment may be inadequate, even dangerous, without concern for the first—which defines the right direction of life for the actor himself. Hence the relevance of Jesus' transition phrase: "The second is like unto it" (the first). Since the lives of few of us represent a perfect fulfillment of the first commandment, does that mean that we should hold in abeyance obedience to the second commandment until the first has been complied with? The answer is obviously negative and for two reasons. The first commandment implies, among other things, the performance of the duties pointed to by the second: the service of God is generally realized in terms of service to neighbor. *And* conscious reflection on what ought to be the true good of the neighbor is an important way of nourishing the best concerns for one's self: here, as in many other ways, the neighbor can be a means of grace to us. Therefore, we can rephrase the injunction, *Love your neighbor as you ought to love yourself,* and, *Do unto others as you ought to want them to do unto you.* (This rephrasing is not an attempt to improve on the words of the Lord; it is merely designed to impart into them more explicitly the context in which they were uttered.)

Thus, simply what my neighbor thinks he wants cannot be the test of my action: perhaps I should do less or more than he wants. A parent does not give a child a pistol no matter how much he wants it, nor should a man accosted in the street give a man with liquor on his breath a quarter "for a cup of coffee," when there is reasonable doubt that the latter is the species of liquid intended to be purchased. In these illustrations the wisdom of the conclusion is obvious enough, but in many other cases the necessary task of discerning the true interest of the other involves the danger of a sort of personal imperialism. One of the symptoms of original sin is that we enjoy "playing God," we enjoy taking over in the lives and affairs of others: A father who holds the purse strings thinks his boy should study business administration; the boy wants to study art. A mother believes that X would be an ideal husband for her daughter; the latter prefers Y. A man wants to borrow one hundred dollars from a friend to go and take a job in Chicago; the friend wants him to take one he has lined up for him in Philadelphia.

How far should we condition our help to others? To what extent should we attempt to influence their directions? Offhand, the most Christian answer would seem to be "Not at all," considering the strong emphasis Christianity puts on freedom and the integrity of the individual. Such an answer would certainly save us from any unwarranted domination of others. But it also relieves us all too easily of our responsibility for the effects of the use of resources at our command. I sin if by a modest gift I put it into the power of a man to become even more intoxicated than I now discern he is. And I sin if I fail to use such gifts of persuasion as I may have to help a person avoid what I sincerely regard as a serious mistake for him.

So even in interpersonal relations a paradox blurs the simplicity of the Golden Rule. Not only must I assess seriously the best interest of the other and devote myself to it; also I must avoid all self-serving eagerness to dominate or to be recognized as "right," and I must positively recognize the importance of the other's autonomy and his uniqueness as a person with needs and potential fulfillments different from mine.

This leads to a basic principle which applies more broadly than to the field under consideration but which is especially significant in relations between individuals, namely, that the personal analogy Our Lord uses ("as thyself"; "unto you") requires more basically than anything else that we treat others as *persons* and not as *things*. They are not to be manipulated, "worked," or "used." Innocently we often betray our violation of this principle in our attitudes: we refer to "the labor market" or say "I got her to . . ."

Actually the finest thing we can do for another is build up his sense of *being a person*. And this we can do in three ways, ways which correspond to our own threefold vocation as made in the image of God—which in turn corresponds to the nature of God Himself as revealed in His relationship to us.

1. We should evoke and inspire the creative possibilities in the other. We should respond appreciatively to his special gifts and draw out of him, by our interest and thoughtful response, the particular talents and winsomeness which may not have adequately received expression. We are called to "build up" people (to use a phrase thought of as slang but actually used by St. Paul in this same context).

2. We should redemptively accept him, though he be rejected by others and perhaps by himself. Here, following the pattern of our Lord, we do not accept the sin but we accept the sinner.

3. We should help bring him into community with others so that he may flower as a person, relating his special characteristics to a wider circle of other personalities to the mutual enrichment and fulfillment of all.

This approach calls for activity as well as restraint. It obviously implies restraint on gossip, which "tears down" the status of persons; on "belittling" the achievements of others, which depresses their self-confidence; on taking unfair advantage of the other's trust of us to advance one's own ends at the expense of the other. But it also implies *active* attention to the needs of other personalities and alertness to opportunities to nourish them and advance their best interests. This positive duty does not require that we must always compliment and never criticize; in fact, our duty often requires candid appraisal. But we should pay special attention to the matter of motive: what we justify as candor is sometimes a ruthless expression of resentment or self-assertiveness—just as our "kind words" of praise may actually be flattery, calculated to further a self-serving purpose.

If we genuinely like the other person all this is natural and easy and well may be the expression of *eros* and *philia* rather than *agapé*. Hence the significance of Jesus' word: "Love your enemies, do good to them that hate you." For it is in the case of the latter that *agapé*—the uniquely Christian love—can be seen in isolation, active in its fullness. This is not to discount *eros* and *philia,* any more than the stress on *agapé* in the case of marriage is meant to discount the role of the other kinds of love. In fact, an act of concern for one alienated from the actor may very well turn his heart and open the way for a *rapprochement* leading to mutual affection.

But if we are rebuffed, how long do we keep trying? Here we have the paradox between Jesus' injunction to shake the dust off the feet and His injunction to forgive "seventy times seven" times. We are always to be open to forgiving, but if we see our overtures are being consistently rejected in one quarter we will quite reasonably, in a sense of vocation, turn elsewhere the energies of our work of reconciliation.

Should we withhold forgiveness of another until he has repented and said he is sorry? Forgiveness, yes—for even God does not forgive till we repent. But *agapé* love, no. We are called to hold ourselves ready to help and maintain our concern, even at the risk of further hurt, following the example of One Who died for us "while we were yet sinners." Here we fulfill the highest norm of all—not only the command, "Love thy neighbor as thyself," but the command, "Love one another as I have loved you."

CHAPTER XV

The Ethics of Business and Profession

Throughout we have seen that the word "vocation" is a key word in Christian ethics. In all that we do, in all the choices that we make, in all the use of our time and resources, we are under a vocation to serve God. But now we turn to the narrower sense of vocation; namely, the question of our calling, the choice of it, and the standards by which we pursue it.

The lives of most of us would be futile if we simply devoted our time to one instance after another of doing good on an *ad hoc* basis. To serve our fellow men best and and—in quite minimum terms—to maintain the rudiments of life in the world, most of us must engage—and should engage—in a regular calling. In a society in which no choice of calling was genuinely afforded people, when men were expected to follow their fathers' calling, the main question was how a given calling could be exercised with dignity and significance under God. But in these times there is a prior question: To what calling ought I to commit myself? If a man is responsible as to each decision he makes to seek to carry out the will of God, then all the more the choice of his major activity in life is under this judgment. Of course we can narrow the field negatively by ruling out those callings which actually do harm to men—the life of a professional burglar, prostitution, etc. But still there is left a wide range of choice among callings which in their main purport serve the legitimate needs and interests of men and thus help in the fulfillment of the will of God and in the advancement of His Kingdom on earth. Once it is recognized that such a decision comes within the range of one's general Christian vocation, and therefore is an ethical decision, then all that can be said about the making of the particular decision would involve simply a repetition of considerations heretofore summarized. We are bound to follow that calling in which we feel we can best serve God. To discern what that is involves everything from an analysis of special aptitude to the particular needs of society during the period in which the decision is being made, as well as the likely possibilities of achieving the result and the means available for doing so. But the Christian faith and ethic has a word particularly applicable to the selection of a calling, which should be kept in mind before and after the choice so that one may properly exercise his functions in the calling, once it is chosen, and properly respect other people's work in our intertwined society under God. Excluding callings which are illegitimate by their very nature, *there is no such thing as a higher or a lower calling.* Religious people naturally tend to feel that the ministry is the highest calling, and, drawing this conclusion, they "downgrade" the calling of every Christian man to serve God to the utmost in that way which seems to him the best opportunity to serve.

The aim at the Reformation was not to cut the ministry "down to size" or to reduce the magnitude of the priestly calling. The aim was to elevate all callings to the level of a ministry and to make the common life holy under God. To conceive of the ministry as the highest calling is to assume that God is interested primarily in religion. But God is interested in having men fed, in having swamps drained, in having disease conquered. God is interested in finishing His creation with our help. God is interested in the redemption of the whole man and not merely of his spirit. So all who build buildings, all who grow food and tend flocks, all who make possible a richer life of the mind and spirit, are engaged in the Divine task of creation and redemption and community building.

But there may be higher and lower vocations for a particular person. Since not all men are gifted with fine, precise minds a man with native scientific abilities has chosen a lower vocation if he becomes a gasoline-station attendant rather than a physicist or chemist. A man able to understand and communicate theology and who is naturally effective as a counsellor of his fellow men will have chosen a lower vocation—for him—if he becomes a bond salesman rather than a minister. But a man who is able most fully to utilize his gifts as a plumber is not in a lower calling than the man who is most fully using his gifts as a clergyman. Both can be ministries—and both can fall short of being ministries. For some clergy the ministry is just a job; for some plumbers the work is a ministry.

Thus once a man has chosen his vocation—the basis of the dedication of his whole self and talents to God—the important question is, Is the man working out his life in that calling as a minister? The first consideration is that of motive. *Why* does he do his work? More important than what he does is why he does it. This is important for his own soul's sake, and in the long run it is also important for the quality of the job. It will also determine in large part the outcome of the second consideration: On what basis does he make his choices within the given calling? Among the various opportunities he may have for action, which does he choose to pursue? As a lawyer or doctor, which cases should he take and which decline? As a

minister, whom should he call on among the hundreds he
could call on? As an inventor, on what projects should he concentrate? Obviously there is no set of rules which can be provided which can cover all cases, nor can such be provided even
by a Christian who is an expert in a given field. Each Christian
is finally thrown back to *ad hoc* decisions, informed by the law
of love.

Even assuming purity of heart and Christian devotion, such
decisions are far from simple. Should a young man in a law
firm work on a case in which the client of the firm is seeking
ends which are legal enough but, in fact, appear to be undesirable as far as society is concerned? Obviously his first duty is
to seek as far as possible to influence his superiors in turn to
influence the client to take another direction. But, failing in
that, he now may not have a chance to make an ideal choice;
rather he may have to choose between two shades of gray. If
he refuses, he may lose the means of livelihood by which he
supports his family (an undoubted obligation) and he may also
lose the opportunity to rise in his profession and thus be a
sound influence on clients as to the direction they should take
in their affairs. On the other hand, if early in his career he
begins limiting his ethical considerations as to whether or not
something is strictly "legal," he may have so hardened himself
to the finer ethical perspectives that, by the time he could be
a person of influence, he may have lost his sense of discrimination. Here, as in many other aspects of life, choices of absolute
black and absolute white are not always offered. In the choices
between grays no man is able to tell another man conclusively
what the will of God is for him or, more accurately, what is less
far from the will of God among two solutions, neither of which
is the perfect will of God. The important thing is that in the
exercise of his vocation a man perceive the nature of the problem and continually seek to transcend the milieu in which he
finds himself, bringing judgment and grace into every situation so

far as he may. If he cannot thus transcend his situation, he is losing one of his most significant possibilities as a human being; he is failing to exercise that quality of transcendence which is the image of God's transcendence. He may find himself merely *used,* which is the ultimate human degradation, rather than *using* his talents to help change the course of things. He is being conformed to the world rather than transforming it. It is possible for a man in one of the "higher" professions actually to exercise it in a way akin to the world's oldest profession.

Are there applicable for each profession or business "middle axioms" which can give general ethical guidance? Most certainly there is room for this level of ethical analysis, but there is no area in which Christian theological and ethical thought has so failed as in this very realm. So-called "legal ethics" or "medical ethics" actually represent minimum "ground rules" developed largely out of prudential and negative considerations, and all too often the maximum there stated becomes the minimum of demand by the individual, by the profession, and by society. It would be comforting for the author to say that in a work of this small compass it is not possible to go into such matters, but the real difficulty is that we have gone a very small distance in providing any answers in this field; thus considerations of space are not the only limitations on the author in this regard. What is needed more than anything today for the redemption of our common life is the gathering together of Christians in each of the principal professions and businesses with theologians and pastors to develop more definite norms of ethics in each of the callings. Nothing would contribute more to the aim of sanctifying each of these callings by impressing upon the practitioners thereof the ministry they are called to exercise, and nothing would do more to provide guidance (though by no means a binding code) for their use in their day-to-day decisions. That there are promising beginnings in this regard in various fields is one of the most encouraging aspects of the present relationship of Christianity to the common life of men.

The same is, of course, true of business and industry. But, even granting, say, a well-thought-out set of "middle axioms" for industry, the fact is that the individual who would seek to follow such norms would be considerably hamstrung by the general economic structure and the mentality governing industry as a whole. Thus it is no accident that Christian thinkers and preachers have been concerned not only with the goodness of the individual layman but with the goodness and soundness of the whole structure within which he operates. The Church has had a long history of concern with the economic, legal, and social order. And, while the Church certainly cannot "back" any given earthly system and make a simple identification of it with the Kingdom of God, Christianity certainly has held before men certain norms by which any system can be judged, on a basis of which modification or reform should be encouraged. Here we can give but a few examples of such principles:

1. While a Christian cannot give unqualified endorsement to "the profit motive" as representing the highest of motives under which men should operate, he can recognize the fact that we are in a fallen world and that, in the maintenance of economic endeavor and persistence in the perennial task of providing a better life for men everywhere, the profit motive is doubtless a necessary one, and systems which would leave it out, while perhaps ideal for men in the Garden of Eden, may not be the best of all situations for men after the Fall.

2. The Christian's task then, in the world as it is, is to seek to interpenetrate and transcend this motive with higher motives, so that the direction of economic activity can be focused not only toward the material ends of greater and greater production and greater and greater income but rather toward the real service of mankind, the real meeting of their needs.

3. The Christian concerned with this field—and all Christians should be—should constantly keep in mind that man is not merely an economic machine. (Even in his work other needs must be met.)

The profit motive, justified on the negative basis of original sin, is not the only basis for the free-enterprise system. There is a much more positive one, more in line with man's original purposes as made in the image of God: the opportunity for creative responsibility. The man who owns his own business obviously has a fuller chance to experiment and to bring to fruition the best results of this thought and imagining. And thus a man so situated is especially stimulated to make the most of this opportunity. That is why many a man will leave a secure position in a large firm and launch out on his own—even with the likelihood of less income. The "profit motive" as such may be an expression of *original sin,* but the urge to be free to create is indubitably an expression of our *creation in the image of God.*

However, the tragedy is that, when free enterprise operates in the form of mass production, ownership and profit-taking become largely separated from the creative function: those who have the ultimate responsibility and control are usually different from those who are called upon to produce. Hence for many the joy and stimulus to creativity is reduced to a minimum; and reduced also to a minimum is the opportunity of viewing one's work as a fulfilling vocation under God. Thus a man's assignment becomes for him a "job" rather than a "calling."

The answer is not in the supplanting of a free-enterprise system with socialism. The latter, though suitable for certain specific situations to be mentioned, in no way ameliorates the principal psychological difficulty of a mass-production and mass-distribution industrial pattern. Nor can we abolish this pattern and return, as some urge, to a simple economic structure. Too many material benefits—meeting the real needs of men—have come from the mass approach. Yet to the degree that, concomitant with such a pattern, factors can be furthered which heighten individual responsibility and freedom to create, not only does the economic pattern become more successful in its own terms, but the spiritual fulfillment of the participants on all levels is enhanced. Whether from the first motive or the second (presumably it is usually a combination of the two), business today is giving increasing attention to this problem, and coming more to the fore are plans whereby employees are permitted to share in the ownership, are given a status which encourages creativity, and are taken more into the counsels of management; and, where possible, smaller, more "personal" units of operation are being developed. The direction of energy toward such solutions is indeed a Christian task for those in a position to further such plans. But ownership and management are sometimes so blinded by the hope of immediate gain and "efficiency" that they will not voluntarily move in these directions. Then it is right for the employees themselves, acting corporately through unions, to bring all legitimate pressure to bear to procure not only a proper minimum share of the profits in the form of wages but also a greater spiritual participation in the enterprise. But since labor unions, to be effective, have to be as plenary as possible, they too suffer from the spiritual dehydration of bigness, with the result that the "rank and file" generally have as little responsibility and voice in union affairs as they do in the affairs of the firms for which they work. Here, too, greater opportunities for participation, responsibility, and creativity are needed.

Such a high valuation upon individuality and free personal fulfillment would seem to argue for the elimination of all elements of state socialism and government control upon free enterprise. It would indeed, if it were not for the fact that there are other economic values to be preserved and furthered, and hence we are forced once again to the task of weighing goods and evils.

First of all, some persons in their creative efforts interfere with other persons' creative opportunities. Hence the necessity

of everything from the policeman on the beat, through munici-
pal zoning regulations, to federal securities regulation.

Second, in an increasingly complicated society increasing
co-ordination of voluntary activities is requisite. Hence the necessity of everything from traffic signals, through the state
licensing of businesses, to federal regulation of the air waves
and air lanes.

Third, owing to "the changes and chances" of even the best
economic order, a floor must be put under the consequences
of economic disaster to the individual. Hence everything from
city clinics, through minimum-wage laws, to governmental un-
employment insurance and old-age benefits.

Fourth, since, in the development of an economic system,
certain essential services cannot feasibly be supplied in a widespread enough way by private firms, government entry into
certain activities becomes necessary. Hence everything from
public parks, roads, and schools to the post office system and
federal electric power development.

And finally, in order to finance all this and to reduce the
extremes of poverty and profits (taking into account the fact
that the fruits of economic success tend to grow in geometric
progression), taxes are imposed—and on a sliding scale related
to income.

Though these tendencies are generally justifiable ethically,
they too involve the government in the problem of mass operation, minimum individual responsibility, and the temptation to
corruption, "respect of persons" and "time-serving," for which
the word "bureaucracy" is a symbol; and all this tends, in
greater or less measure, to delimit the *good* creative expression
of the individual as well as the *evil*.

Obviously, then, the more individuals, firms, and groups of
businesses can voluntarily assume these various positive functions, and the more they can by voluntary discipline regulate
themselves, the more the functions of government should be
progressively reduced. In the simplest individual terms, the

more people that behave themselves and work out their salvation with helpfulness rather than harm to others, the fewer policemen we will need. And, by similar token, the more industry finds ways of insuring adequate security to its participants, the less provision for public security is needed. And the more energetic private finance is about developing low-cost housing, the less public housing will be needed. And the more universal full disclosure of the facts in the offering of securities, the smaller the staff of the Securities and Exchange Commission need be. But, meanwhile, simply to say that big government represents an evil and private enterprise should be unhampered is to presuppose man before the Fall. If there ever was such a man, in historic terms, he cannot be precisely identified as the modern entrepreneur—or labor unionist—or bureaucrat.

CHAPTER XVI

Toward Doing the Truth

Ethics doesn't "just come natural." Original sin is the shorthand way of saying why regard for self often keeps us from meeting *known* needs of others and preoccupation with self often keeps us from even *knowing* the needs. True, the Christian who has experienced and continues to experience justification has a dynamic for goodness which is especially effective in overriding the claims of self. But it is not automatic, for, as the Anglican Articles of Religion remind us, "This infection of nature doth remain, yea in them that are regenerated."

There is, of course, a natural joy in doing good. This actual experience of man is sufficient to contradict the notion of "total depravity" (unless one defines this very carefully—as "in every part" rather than "entirely" depraved). The image of God is entirely defaced in no man, and indeed behavior consonant therewith is given an especially effective motive in the thanksgiving for forgiveness. But the old Adam is there in each of us, along with the new Adam. So, granting knowledge of the law and granting justification, we still find it difficult consistently to do what we know we should do—and what one aspect of our being actually *wants* to do. It was the converted Paul, not the unregenerate Saul, who cried, "Those things that I would do, I don't do, and those things I would not do, I do."

Some regard an honest recognition of our proclivity to sin as "cutting the nerve of moral effort." This criticism overlooks the fact that the sense of gratitude for forgiven sin provides a spur to moral effort even greater than confidence in one's own moral capabilities. But actually a candid recognition of "the other side" of our nature is not for a moment proposed as an excuse for sin: In the Christian "scheme of salvation" the responsibility for perfection is asserted right alongside the realistic recognition of the universality of original sin and the tendencies which this concept represents. Further—and this is our main point here—this recognition alerts us to the importance of making conscious efforts to safeguard ourselves from our own sinful tendencies. The child who fears fire is less likely to be burned than the one not aware of its dangers.

Here then we consider those ways and means whereby we can strengthen the will to goodness and counteract our tendency to evil. It might appear to some that such considerations have no place in a book on Christian ethics, in which we are concerned rather with what our duty is. But the fact is, as was indicated in the chapter on worship, that we do have an ethical duty to do those things which will assist us in the performance of our other ethical obligations. If I have an obligation to pay a man next year it may be a present obligation to save money this year. Likewise in regard to my continuing ethical obligations, I am under duty to illumine my mind and strengthen my will in ways which will make it most likely that I will perform these duties.

In this regard the mind presents a less complex problem than the will, at least in theory; i.e., when conceived as seeking the truth as to what is right apart from the overt or covert deflections of the will. Hence we will discuss the mental aspect first and more briefly.

Serious attention to a specific ethical decision generally requires a syllogism: *a major premise* which embodies the principle or principles involved, *a minor premise* which includes the relevant facts, and *a conclusion* therefrom. A perception of the principles is not something automatic: our minds and consciences do not so work. Our awareness of the principles at stake depends upon the degree to which we have furnished our minds and trained our consciences with the cumulative results of the experience of the people of God in seeking to do the truth. The Bible, Old and New Testaments, is obviously paramount. We cannot use the Bible as an "answer book" in relation to particular ethical questions; but it does manifest throughout, in "divers manners and sundry places," the meaning of vocation under God, the scope of obligation, the scale of priorities, the importance of motive, the inner character of goodness, the danger of rationalization, and the drama of the redemption which is the dynamic for goodness. But the Holy Spirit has not been inactive since the close of the Canon of Scripture: the work of revelation of the will of God continues, in the lives of the saints, the word of the prophets and reformers of all times, the thoughtful analyses of dedicated scholars, the continuing voice of the liturgies of many traditions, the contemporary voice of the preachers from thousands of pulpits. Participation, as far as may be, in this whole expression of experience and thought is the best way to develop a reservoir of insight available when particular decisions have to be made. *Thus one can think as a Christian.* Too often Christians, with the best motives in the world, actually think as secularists in relation to personal and social problems. But our obligation to think as Christians does not require that our minds should be closed to secular analyses of the human task. The Holy Spirit operates through many who do not acknowledge His working in the world. And especially should we be attentive to secular critiques of Christian thought, policy, and action. God may be thereby speaking to the Church, and by closing our ears through a supposed loyalty to Christianity we may perchance be closing our ears to the voice of God.

If then such study, thought, and attentiveness are a means toward the acceptance of the right major premises, then this activity is *itself* among our positive ethical duties.

To provide sound minor premises for our syllogisms of decision we need the facts. Few of us can maintain a private research staff for the assembling of the facts in a given situation, and in any case much that would be relevant data—in both interpersonal and public realms—is just not available. *But we are called upon to find out what we can and be open to what we find.* Rarely can either of these elements be improvised. The latter—the openness—is a bent of mind, a passion for the truth. The former—the finding—depends upon an alertness over the years. The cultivation of a zest for facts and of freedom from prepossession is a lifelong task, and knowing the facts of a given issue is not just the work of the day we have to decide it.

If then the cultivation of objectivity and the accumulation of relevant information are means toward the right minor premises, then this activity is *itself* among our positive ethical duties.

So much for the mind. How can the will to goodness be fortified and strengthened? In other words, *how can we better resist temptation?*

Throughout most of Christian history temptation has been conceived of as a whispering to the soul on the part of the devil or one of his agents. While it would be difficult—and, in fact, is quite unnecessary—to accept this view of the matter literally, it is by no means as naïve as it would appear. The devil has never been pictured as suggesting something "out of the blue"; rather he is seen as pressing to the fore those interests which are already impressive either in the background of the person tempted or in the milieu around him. Further, the devil has always been viewed as quite capable of using earthly associates (innocent or otherwise), and usually, whether working through others or directly, he is not pictured as suggesting to the soul that it do evil but rather that the evil is in fact good, or at least not *very* evil. Often the devil's work is seen as most effective in leading the mind to focus upon a particular interest (sometimes even a valid one) to the exclusion of others. Thus, though today we are likely to re-interpret all of this in psychological and sociological terms, we have to take into account the same factors as are present in the older imagery.

The classic illustration is Jesus' temptation in the wilderness. Now conscious of His Messiahship (presumably from the time of the baptism by John), Jesus draws apart to focus on the direction of His vocation as Messiah. What the devil brings to His mind, successively, are the principal popular Messianic expectations of His countrymen, roles which in fact would appeal to Jesus as man, and roles which He had already sensed His capacity to fulfill.

First it is suggested that He provide an economic solution: "Command that these stones be made bread." A Messianic fulfillment in terms of a land of plenty had genuine roots in the tradition and represented a valid interest for God's people. That He Himself, at the proper time, recognized this interest is pictured in the narratives of the feeding of the multitude. Second, it is suggested that He express the Messianic fulfillment in terms of wonders to delight the popular thirst for magic and supernatural display: "Then the devil taketh Him up into the Holy City, and setteth Him upon a pinnacle of the Temple, and saith unto Him, If Thou be the Son of God cast thyself down." That God does in fact work mighty wonders is also a valid part of the biblical tradition. Third, a powerful earthly ruler fitted in with many of the Messianic predictions: "Again the devil taketh Him up into an exceeding high mountain, and showeth Him all the kingdoms of the world, and the glory of them; and saith unto Him, All these things will I give thee." So all three of these temptations take the form of plausible directions of vocation, both in terms of a man's natural taste and in terms of social acceptance.

In replying to the devil our Lord perceives in each case precisely what is wrong with making any one of the three the direction for His life. He does not imply that the material well-being of man is unimportant: He points out that man cannot live by bread *alone;* thus He has to put first things first; i.e., the conversion of the spirit of men, the bringing in of the kingdom of God on spiritual foundations. And obviously He is not averse to miracle; but He refuses to "give a sign" for the sake of a display, in contravention of the normal law of gravitation: "Thou shalt not tempt the Lord thy God." And He recognizes the place of governmental authority ("Render unto Caesar . . ."), but He perceives that the price of making political domination an end in itself is the worship of the devil, that God with His larger claims stands above all political arrangements: "Thou shalt worship the Lord thy God and Him only shalt thou serve."

Generally temptation is an attraction to *oversimplification:* when we focus our attention on a particular aim we very easily overlook other aims and interests which have to be weighed in the balance under the overarching sovereignty of God. Suppose at a house party a man has a convenient opportunity to effect a night's liaison with an attractive woman, who is similarly tempted. Actually the urge to sensual fulfillment is in itself a good thing and the temptation will be buttressed by the suggestion his mind readily provides: it will do no harm to anybody. Even if he is married he may honor such a suggestion ("no harm to anybody"), saying to himself that he doesn't mean this seriously anyway and it will in no way affect his relationship with his wife, to whom he wishes to have nothing but the highest loyalty. What his passion and power of rationalization tend to crowd out are considerations which are obvious enough in a calmer light: the risk of the actual defection of his own affections from the one to whom, under God, he has committed himself for life; the risk that the sentiments of his partner may be focused upon him in a way that she does not anticipate (the fact that people *say* they are "not serious" does not necessarily mean that nothing serious can in effect develop in their affections), and the risk that the matter may result in a direct hurt to his wife—perhaps one devastating to the marriage and the bases of trust in it. And some of these considerations apply even if both are single.

Connected with this tendency to oversimplification is a corollary factor: a tendency to *preoccupation*. One's life and all the factors in it are like a great mural. In our finiteness we tend to focus the light on one portion of it or another and, by a sort of metonymy in reverse, conceive the part to be the whole. To continue the illustration used above, people who hear of an instance of adultery often ask, "How could he have done such a thing?" Perhaps not always, but generally, such sins are not merely "slips"; they are not momentary, unexplainable aberrations. Usually there is a background of preoccupation with thoughts of sexual fulfillment, a developed eagerness for variety or what is supposed might be a greater satisfaction. This is why in the Catholic penitential system there is explicit concern for the matter of "unclean thoughts." In Roman Catholic moral theology it is taught, for example, that an unclean thought freely consented to is a mortal sin, not a venial one (if it is not freely consented to it is no sin at all, but if it is adjudged sin it is characterized as mortal). This teaching has created in many people "scruples" which are psychologically and morally quite undesirable. This may explain the almost complete inattention to this matter on the part of Protestant moral theologians, preachers, and counselors. While the distinction between categories of "mortal" and of "venial" sins is not particularly fruitful, nevertheless it is most certainly true that we are influenced by the impressions with which we have stocked our conscious and unconscious minds. This is in part the meaning of "fixation." For example, it is now being generally recognized that horror comics have a relationship to delinquency because they keep underlining for their readers cruelty and lust. So do any preoccupations in our thoughts weaken the resistance when specific opportunities for sin arise. Thus, if adultery is a sin, thoughts of illicit sex are also sinful: it is this that lies behind our Lord's word, "Whosoever looketh on a woman to lust after her hath committed adultery with her already in his heart." This position need not be justified in terms of an abstract requirement of purity of thought but simply in terms of our general effort to do those things which contribute to our ability to fulfill the specific will of God as to our neighbors and to avoid those things which detract from our ability to do so.

The process of fixation can also be seen in the field of homosexuality. While we are far from having an adequate understanding in this field or a widely successful therapy, it is evident that the deviation in pattern often results from an early focusing of preoccupation, usually under the influence of others, whereby members of the same sex become in *mind*—and hence in the *action* of the people thus affected—a paramount avenue of fulfillment in contrast to the normal means of sexual enjoyment. Through this fixation a vicious cycle is set up: the more the special conduct is indulged in the more intense the thought thereupon, and vice versa. And an even more vivid example of the results of preoccupation, which is in turn fed by action, is furnished by various forms of fetishism.

Though examples have been taken from the sexual fields, because the implications are there more readily apparent, the same thing applies to false emphases of all sorts—greed for money, lust for power, a priority of social prestige over all other claims, overemphasis upon various recreational possibilities.

This latter example especially reminds us that the injunction about the control of our thoughts and preoccupations is not merely a negative one. The trouble with daydreaming about something that will contribute to our being led astray is basically that during that time our minds are *not* focused upon those things which will lead us aright. The right use of our time, the normal fulfillments of our nature, the proper expression of vocation depend in large measure on what, in our moments of reflection, we have furnished our minds with. If we have nourished the heart with good things then more and more we *want* to do the right things.

But the complication of our nature is such that, in spite of the most positive concern for those thoughts and experiences which make for right motivation and right action, we nevertheless have difficulty in deciding for the right if alluring contrary possibilities are presented to us. Therefore, in the principal religious traditions a pattern of discipline has generally been encouraged by which we accustom ourselves to conform in realms which do not in themselves seem to present moral issues in order that we may thus strengthen our responses to what we deem right. Perhaps we can make the point first by choosing an example unrelated to typical ecclesiastical disciplines. Some people choose to stop smoking as the first step in a program of losing weight. At first blush this would seem odd, since smoking generally decreases the appetite and, as a matter of fact, when this step is taken there is sometimes an initial gain in weight. However, their explanation is that by stopping smoking they accustom themselves to disciplining their appetites and thus gain the strength to stop drinking (thereby curtailing calories) and finally—the hardest of all—to stop eating too much food. Likewise a rule of life, either a personal one or one that is traditional with a man's particular religious allegiance, can accustom us to respond to discipline in the realm of our appetites and thus help strengthen the will.

We are on dangerous ground here, because associated with the thought of particular rules of discipline has often been a legalism confining the meaning of the moral law to the keeping of the observances of the tradition. These rules can become an end in themselves—even sometimes interfering, as we have seen, with performance of "the weightier matters of the law." Thus the tendency of the Protestant Churches has been to sweep away such traditional schemes of discipline. These factors are illustrated in the familiar story of a long-deferred penitent who confessed to a Roman Catholic priest, in response to the latter's questions, that he had engaged in murder, theft, lying, and adultery, but who to a final question, "Have you eaten meat on Friday?" replied, "What do you think I am, a —— Protestant?"

Yet there is a place for regular patterns of discipline, provided they are viewed as instrumental and always subject to direct contradiction by particular claims of the law of love. To be specific, it would be quite proper for a person to decide not to eat meat on Friday, the day of our Lord's death on Calvary, both as a regular reminder of that mighty act for our salvation and as a means of strengthening his responses to more substantive claims laid upon him—*provided* one did not associate his performance of this rule with moral achievement *per se* or woodenly adhere to it in the face of the sensitivities of one's hostess or at the expense of the actual waste of food. Further, if any such rule is to operate as a governance of the flesh there is no particular value in a legalism which allows the substitution of lobster for hamburger meat.

The same considerations apply in the case of days of fasting, set hours for meditation, and set days for worship, as well as fasting before Holy Communion. In the case of the latter, for example, a proper (but not overweening) concern for one's health is, of course, a prior ethical claim over the instrumental value of the discipline, and the fasting should not be regarded as more important than the receiving.

Further, since these disciplines are instrumental, they are not themselves things to be witnessed to, as are the things of the Gospel. The means by which one can better be enabled to do good and avoid evil are wisely kept a private matter; the good works themselves, if they result, and one's witness to convictions which underlie a life of goodness, will sufficiently commend the Master of our lives. Thus our Lord's word: "When ye fast, be not, as the hypocrites, of a sad countenance: for they disfigure their faces, that they may appear unto men to fast. Verily I say unto you, they have their reward. But thou, when thou fastest, anoint thine head and wash thy face, that thou appear not unto men to fast. . . ."

Obviously the greatest instrumental means for avoiding preoccupation, widening our horizons, and strengthening our wills are *worship and prayer,* which, as we have already seen, are both instrumental and of primary substantive value and meaning in themselves. We have already discussed the ethical requirement of worship (and, since the two cannot be really separated, of prayer); we should now consider the ways in which *prayer* particularly can aid our whole moral response.

The first thing prayer can do is to bring us consciously into the presence of God. This in itself brings into the balance, as we make decisions, the most powerful and significant aspect of our lives, but which even ordinarily decent people often leave out in making their decisions. The fact that *God is* makes all the difference in regard to most moral choices. A consistent sense of the presence of God carries over from our conscious acts of prayer to our daily activities and to our daily decidings.

Second, prayer sorts out and judges our intentions. If we pray honestly as to what we want and yearn for, we will find that there are some things we cannot really pray for. Something that we cannot in good conscience pray for we cannot in good conscience want. The public prayer of corporate worship sets before us ends and aims that we *ought* to have: we should be concerned for the sick and the suffering and the underprivileged, for the peace of the world, etc. But our private prayer, to be sincere, should set forth only what we really *do* want and are willing to work for. Thus, if we find that our private prayer has too narrow a scope, that is a judgment upon the actual narrowness of our interests and concerns. More specifically, as to temptation, God in response to prayer actually gives us an increase of grace to meet it, nourishing in us the positive factors and interests which can outweigh the negative pulls: "My grace is sufficient for thee" is His word.

And, finally, if we constantly rely on prayer in connection with our daily activities and choices we will be saved from the temptation of a sense of self-sufficiency: the well-worn adage is still significant: "Pride goeth before a fall."

We see the scope of this relationship between prayer and goodness in the traditional analysis of the kinds of prayer. In *adoration* we call to mind the fact of God and who God is, thus providing the setting for His claim upon us and bringing Him to the fore in the factors involved in decision. In the prayer of *penitence* we pause to recognize the fact of our sins. Such prayers are of little value if they merely express a general mood of sinfulness. They should be based upon and preceded by regular examination of conscience so that we judge ourselves by what at least is a shadow of God's judgment of us. And, to be effective, this discipline should be regular, not merely a reverie we indulge in when we feel particularly sinful. In prayers of *thanksgiving* we strengthen the motive which is the dynamic for goodness and extend the base of its power as we recall "our creation, preservation, and all the blessings of this life; but above all, thine inestimable love in the redemption of the world by our Lord Jesus Christ; the means of grace, and the hope of glory." Thus we seek "that due sense of thy mercy, that our hearts may be unfeignedly thankful; and that we may show forth thy praise, not only with our lips, but in our lives, by giving up ourselves to thy service, and by walking before thee in holiness and righteousness all our days." In prayers of *petition* we focus the direction of our action, as especially concerns ourselves; and in our prayer of *intercession* we call to mind the various claims upon us which take the form of the needs of others. And in the form of prayer we so often neglect—the prayer of *silence*—we give God the Holy Spirit the opportunity to speak directly to us, in compunction for the past and in guidance for the future. Even when rational analysis of relative goods and evils reaches no clear conclusion His voice can speak to us unequivocally.

So in regard to the most important support for a life under the law of God—that is, for the fulfilling of our vocation—it is God first and man second. We are not fully ourselves or fulfilled even in earthly terms unless we live day by day under charter from Him, constantly returning to Him for illumination as to the truth about life, for the grace of acceptance when we have not lived according to the truth, and for continual aid and support in our renewed efforts—in gratitude—to do the truth.